P9-DFJ-430

KEEP CALM

AND

SLOW COOK

KEEP
CALM
AND
SLOW
COOK

THUNDER BAY
P·R·E·S·S

Thunder Bay Press
An imprint of the Baker & Taylor Publishing Group
10350 Barnes Canyon Road, San Diego, CA 92121
www.thunderbaybooks.com

Copyright © 2014 The National Magazine Company Limited and Collins & Brown

Produced by Collins & Brown
an imprint of Anova Books Company Ltd.,
10 Southcombe Street, London W14 0RA, U.K.

Copyright under International, Pan American, and Universal Copyright
Conventions. All rights reserved. No part of this book may be reproduced or
transmitted in any form or by any means, electronic or mechanical, including
photocopying, recording, or by any information storage-and-retrieval system,
without written permission from the copyright holder. Brief passages (not to
exceed 1,000 words) may be quoted for reviews.

"Thunder Bay" is a registered trademark of Baker & Taylor. All rights reserved.

All notations of errors or omissions should be addressed to Thunder Bay Press,
Editorial Department, at the above address. All other correspondence (author
inquiries, permissions) concerning the content of this book should be addressed
to Collins & Brown Old Magistrates Court, 10 Southcombe Street, London,
W14 0RA, U.K.

ISBN-13: 978-1-60710-926-6
ISBN-10: 1-60710-926-3

Library of Congress Cataloging-in-Publication Data

Dixon, Barbara (Barbara Elizabeth)
Keep calm and slow cook / Barbara Dixon.
    pages cm
ISBN 978-1-60710-926-6 -- ISBN 1-60710-926-3
1. Electric cooking, Slow. I. Title.
TX827.B38 2013
641.5'884--dc23
                                2013024470

Printed in China

2 3 4 5 17 16 15 14

Cover illustration by Emma Kelly

Photographers: Neil Barclay (pages 45, 69, 70,
74, 79, 88, 108, 142, 171, and 176); Martin
Brigdale (pages 50, 150, 153, and 175); Nicki
Dowey (pages 11, 13, 18, 19, 21, 22, 24, 27,
29, 33, 35, 36, 37, 38, 43, 44, 49, 62, 67, 73,
78, 85, 93, 97, 110, 113, 116, 119, 120, 123,
125, 126, 137, 138, 146, 149, 154, 155, 157,
159, 161, 163, 164, 172, 181, 182, 185, 189,
190, 192, 195, 197, 198, 201, 202, 203, 206,
207, 209, 211, 213, 214, 223, 226, 228, 231,
235, and 236); Will Heap (page 133); Craig
Robertson (pages 8, 14, 16, 17, 25, 30, 47, 53,
61, 77, 83, 87, 89, 90, 90, 95, 98, 99, 103,
106, 107, 128, 129, 130, 121, 134, 151 186,
200, 217, 219, 220, 225, and 233); Lucinda
Symons (pages 55, 56, 65, 105, 145, 167,
and 169); Martin Thompson (page 101)

Home Economists: Joanna Farrow,
Emma Jane Frost, Teresa Goldfinch, Alice Hart,
Anna Burges-Lumsden, Lucy McKelvie,
Kim Morphew, Katie Rogers, Bridget Sargeson,
Sarah Tildesley, Jennifer White and
Mari Mererid Williams

Stylists: Susanna Blake, Wei Tang,
Sarah Tildesley, Helen Trent and Fanny Ward

Notes

All spoon measures are level.
1 teaspoon = 5ml spoon; 1 tablespoon = 15ml spoon.
Ovens and broilers must be preheated to the specified temperature.
Large eggs should be used except where otherwise specified.

Dietary Guidelines

Note that certain recipes contain raw or lightly cooked eggs. The young, elderly,
pregnant women, and anyone with immune-deficiency disease should avoid these
because of the slight risk of salmonella.
Note that some recipes contain alcohol. Check the ingredients list before serving
to children.

Contents

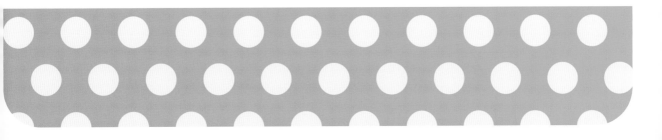

TASTY
SOUPS

Seafood Gumbo

Preparation Time 10 minutes • Cooking Time 30 minutes • Serves 4 • Per Serving 559 calories, 23g fat (3g saturated), 58g carbohydrates, 1,200mg sodium • Easy

½ cup (1 stick) butter
⅓ cup all-purpose flour
1–2 tablespoons Cajun spice mix
1 onion, chopped
1 green bell pepper, seeded and chopped
5 scallions, sliced
1 tablespoon freshly chopped Italian parsley
1 garlic clove, crushed
1 beefsteak tomato, chopped
4 ounces Italian-style garlic sausage, finely sliced

⅓ cup instant white rice
4½ cups vegetable stock
1 pound okra, sliced
1 bay leaf
1 fresh thyme sprig
2 teaspoons salt
¼ teaspoon cayenne pepper
juice of ½ lemon
4 cloves
1 pound frozen mixed seafood (containing mussels, squid, and shrimp), thawed and drained
ground black pepper

1. Heat the butter in a 2½-quart heavy saucepan over low heat. Add the flour and Cajun spice and cook, stirring, for 1–2 minutes, until golden brown. Add the onion, green bell pepper, scallions, parsley, and garlic. Cook for 5 minutes.

2. Add the tomato, garlic sausage, and rice to the pan and stir well to coat. Add the stock, okra, bay leaf, thyme, salt, cayenne pepper, lemon juice, and cloves. Season with black pepper. Bring to a boil. Then reduce the heat and simmer, covered, for 12 minutes or until the rice is tender.

3. Add the seafood and cook for 2 minutes to heat through. Serve the gumbo in deep bowls.

COOK'S TIP
Gumbo is a traditional stew from the South, using meat, vegetables, and shellfish and thickened with okra.

Fall Vegetable Soup

Preparation Time 15 minutes • Cooking Time 45 minutes • Serves 4 • Per Serving 326 calories, 17g fat (9g saturated), 29g carbohydrates, 1,100mg sodium • Easy

4 tablespoons butter

1 medium onion, diced

4 red-skinned or white round potatoes, diced

4 ounces bacon, diced

1 garlic clove, chopped

1 cup chopped white of leek

2 Pippin apples, unpeeled, cored, and chopped

2 teaspoons dried thyme

1 teaspoon dill seeds (optional)

2½ cups dry cider

3½ cups hot vegetable stock

1¼ cups shredded savoy cabbage

salt and ground black pepper

1. Melt the butter in a large saucepan. Add the onion, potatoes, bacon, garlic, leek, apples, thyme, and dill seeds, if using. Season to taste with salt and black pepper, stir and then cover the pan and cook gently for 15 minutes.

2. Add the cider and bring to a boil. Then reduce the heat and simmer for 5 minutes. Add the hot stock and simmer for about 15 minutes or until the potatoes are soft.

3. Pour half the soup into a blender or liquidizer and blend until smooth. Add to the remaining soup in the pan. Reheat gently, add the shredded cabbage, and simmer for another 3 minutes. Ladle into warmed bowls and serve straight away.

Winter Minestrone

Preparation Time 10 minutes • Cooking Time 45 minutes • Serves 4 • Per Serving 334 calories, 11g fat (3g saturated), 47g carbohydrates, 1,500mg sodium • Dairy Free • Easy

2 tablespoons olive oil

1 small onion, finely chopped

1 carrot, chopped

1 celery stick, chopped

1 garlic clove, crushed

2 tablespoons freshly chopped thyme

4 cups vegetable stock

1 (14½-ounce) can diced tomatoes

1 (15-ounce) can chickpeas, drained and rinsed

1 cup minestrone pasta

1¾ cups shredded savoy cabbage

salt and ground black pepper

fresh ready-made pesto (see Cook's Tip on page 23), toasted ciabatta, and extra virgin olive oil to serve

1. Heat the oil in a large saucepan and add the onion, carrot, and celery. Cook for 8–10 minutes, until softened. Then add the garlic and thyme. Sauté for another 2–3 minutes.

2. Add the stock, tomatoes, and half the chickpeas and bring to a boil. Mash the remaining chickpeas and stir into the soup. Then reduce the heat and simmer for 30 minutes, adding the minestrone pasta and cabbage for the last 10 minutes of cooking time.

3. Check the seasoning and correct, if necessary. Ladle into warmed bowls and serve with a dollop of fresh pesto on top and slices of toasted ciabatta drizzled with extra virgin olive oil on the side.

Classic Fish Soup

Preparation Time 10 minutes • Cooking Time about 15 minutes • Serves 4 • Per Serving 269 calories, 10g fat (2g saturated), 6g carbohydrates, 400mg sodium • Gluten Free • Dairy Free • Easy

3 tablespoons olive oil

1 leek, trimmed and finely chopped

4 fat garlic cloves, crushed

3 celery sticks, finely chopped

1 small fennel bulb, finely chopped

1 red chili, seeded and finely chopped (see Cook's Tip)

4½ cups boiling water

¼ cup dry white wine*

1¾ pounds mixed fish and shellfish (such as cod, halibut and red snapper fillets), peeled and deveined uncooked shrimp, and fresh mussels, scrubbed, and cleaned (see Cook's Tip on page 52)

4 tomatoes, chopped

½ cup freshly chopped thyme

salt and ground black pepper

1. Heat the oil a large saucepan and add the leek, garlic, celery, fennel, and chili. Cook over medium heat for 5 minutes or until the vegetables are soft and beginning to brown.

2. Stir in the boiling water and the wine. Bring to a boil, and then reduce the heat, cover the pan, and simmer for 5 minutes.

3. Cut the white fish into large chunks. Add to the soup with the tomatoes and thyme. Continue to simmer gently until the fish has just turned opaque. Add the shrimp, simmer for 1 minute, and then add the mussels, if you're using them.

4. As soon as all the mussels have opened (discard any that do not), season the soup with salt and black pepper. Ladle into warmed bowls and serve immediately.

* This recipe is not suitable for children because it contains alcohol.

TRY SOMETHING DIFFERENT

To give the soup more of a kick, stir in 2 tablespoons Pernod instead of the wine. Garlic croutons are traditionally served with fish soup; they can be made while the soup is simmering. Toast small slices of baguette, spread with garlic mayonnaise, and sprinkle with grated cheese. Float in the hot soup just before serving.

COOK'S TIP

Chilies vary greatly in strength, from mild to blistering hot, depending on the type of chili and its ripeness. Taste a small piece first to check that it's not too spicy. You can reduce the hotness by removing the seeds and pith. When handling chilies, be extremely careful not to touch or rub your eyes with your fingers because it will make them sting. Wash knives immediately after chopping chilies. As a precaution, use rubber gloves when preparing them, if desired.

Summer Vegetable Soup with Herb Pistou

Preparation Time 20 minutes • Cooking Time 1 hour • Serves 6 • Per Serving 163 calories,
7g fat (1g saturated), 17g carbohydrates, 100mg sodium • Vegetarian • Gluten Free • Dairy Free • Easy

3 tablespoons sunflower oil
1 onion, finely chopped
**2 red-skinned or white round
   potatoes, finely diced**
3 carrots, finely diced
1 turnip, finely diced
6 cups cold water
4 bay leaves
6 large fresh sage leaves
2 small zucchini, finely diced
**6 ounces green beans, trimmed
   and halved**

¾ cup shelled small peas
**2 tomatoes, seeded and finely
   diced**
**1 small head broccoli, broken into
   florets**
salt and ground black pepper
**pistou (see Cook's Tip) or ready-
   made pesto (see Cook's Tip on
   page 23) to serve**

1. Heat the oil in a large saucepan over gentle heat. Add the onion, potatoes, carrots, and turnip and cook for 10 minutes. Pour in the cold water, season with salt and black pepper, bring to a boil, and add the bay and sage leaves. Reduce the heat and simmer for 25 minutes.

2. Add the zucchini, beans, peas, and tomatoes. Bring back to a boil and simmer for 10–15 minutes. Add the broccoli 5 minutes before the end of the cooking time.

3. Remove the bay and sage leaves and adjust the seasoning if needed. Pour the soup into warmed bowls and serve immediately; serve the pistou or pesto separately to stir into the hot soup.

COOK'S TIP

Pistou is a Provençal condiment similar to Italian pesto. To make your own, use a mortar and pestle, a small bowl and the end of a rolling pin, or a mini processor. Pound together ¾ teaspoon sea salt and 6 chopped garlic cloves until smooth. Add ¼ cup freshly chopped basil and pound to a paste, then mix in ¾ cup olive oil, a little at a time. Store in a sealed jar in the refrigerator for up to 1 week.

Smoked Cod and Corn Chowder

Preparation Time 5 minutes • Cooking Time 20 minutes • Serves 6 • Per Serving 517 calories, 28g fat (15g saturated), 35g carbohydrates, 4,700mg sodium • Easy

4½ ounces cubed pancetta or bacon

4 tablespoons butter

3 leeks, trimmed and thinly sliced

¼ cup all-purpose flour

2½ cups reduced fat or whole milk

1¼ cups cold water

1½ pounds undyed smoked cod loin or haddock, skinned and cut into ¾-inch cubes

1 (11-ounce) can corn kernels in water, drained

1 pound small new potatoes, sliced

⅔ cup heavy cream

½ teaspoon paprika

salt and ground black pepper

2 tablespoons freshly chopped Italian parsley to garnish

1. Sauté the pancetta or bacon in a large saucepan over gentle heat until the fat runs out. Add the butter to the pan to melt. Add the leeks and cook until softened.

2. Stir in the flour and cook for a few seconds, then pour in the milk and the cold water. Add the fish to the pan with the corn and potatoes. Bring to a boil, and then reduce the heat and simmer for 10–15 minutes, until the potatoes are cooked.

3. Stir in the cream, season with salt, black pepper, and paprika, and cook for 2–3 minutes to warm through. Ladle into warmed shallow bowls and sprinkle each one with a little chopped parsley. Serve immediately.

Spicy Bean and Zucchini Soup

Preparation Time 10 minutes • Cooking Time 30 minutes • Serves 4 • Per Serving 289 calories,
8g fat (1g saturated), 43g carbohydrates, 1,500mg sodium • Vegetarian • Dairy Free • Easy

2 tablespoons olive oil
1 medium onion, finely chopped
2 garlic cloves, crushed
2 teaspoons ground coriander
1 tablespoon paprika
1 teaspoon mild curry powder
3 zucchini, trimmed, halved,
   and sliced
2 red-skinned or white round
   potatoes, diced

1 (15-ounce) can red kidney beans,
   drained and rinsed
1 (15-ounce) can great Northern
   beans, drained and rinsed
6⅓ cups vegetable stock
salt and ground black pepper
crusty bread to serve

1. Heat the oil in a saucepan. Add the onions and garlic and sauté for 2 minutes. Add the spices and cook, stirring, for 1 minute. Mix in the zucchini and potatoes and cook for 1–2 minutes.

2. Add the remaining ingredients and bring to a boil. Reduce the heat, cover the pan, and simmer for 25 minutes, stirring occasionally, or until the potatoes are tender. Adjust the seasoning, if necessary.

3. Ladle into warmed bowls and serve with crusty bread.

COOK'S TIP
Look for medium, firm zucchini. They lose their flavor as they grow.

Vegetable Barley Soup

Preparation Time 10 minutes • Cooking Time 1 hour 5 minutes • Serves 4 • Per Serving 86 calories, trace fat (0g saturated), 17g carbohydrates, 100mg sodium • Vegetarian • Dairy Free • Easy

2 tablespoons barley, washed and drained
4 cups vegetable stock
2 large carrots, diced
1 turnip, diced
2 leeks, trimmed and sliced
2 celery sticks, diced
1 small onion, finely chopped
1 bouquet garni (see Cook's Tip)
2 tablespoons freshly chopped parsley
salt and ground black pepper

1. Put the barley and stock into a saucepan and bring to a boil. Reduce the heat and simmer for 45 minutes or until the barley is cooked and tender.

2. Add the vegetables to the pan with the bouquet garni and season to taste with black pepper. Bring to a boil, and then reduce the heat and simmer for about 20 minutes or until the vegetables are tender.

3. Discard the bouquet garni. Add the parsley to the soup, season to taste with salt and black pepper, and stir well. Ladle into warmed bowls and serve immediately.

COOK'S TIP
To make a bouquet garni, use kitchen string to tie together a sprig each of fresh thyme and parsley with a bay leaf and a piece of celery.

Spicy Lamb Soup

Preparation Time 15 minutes • Cooking Time about 1 hour • Serves 4 • Per serving 367 calories, 17g fat (6g saturated), 31g carbohydrates, 600mg sodium • Gluten Free • Dairy Free • Easy

1 tablespoon olive oil
12 ounces ground lamb
1 medium onion, finely chopped
1 cup canned tomatoes
3 teaspoons harissa paste
6⅓ cups hot lamb stock
½ cup couscous
1 (15-ounce) can chickpeas, drained and rinsed
salt and ground black pepper
1 tablespoon each freshly chopped Italian parsley and mint to garnish
flatbread and lemon wedges to serve (optional)

1. Heat half the oil in a large saucepan and brown the ground lamb in batches. Set aside.

2. Add the remaining oil and gently sauté the onion for 10 minutes or until softened. Add the tomatoes and harissa and simmer, covered, for 30 minutes.

3. Add the hot stock and couscous and simmer for 10 minutes. Stir in the chickpeas and heat through for 2–3 minutes. Add the herbs and check the seasoning. Serve immediately with warmed flatbread and lemon wedges, if desired, to squeeze into the soup.

GET AHEAD

To prepare ahead Complete the recipe to the end of step 2. Cool, cover, and chill for up to three days. *To use* Complete the recipe.

Pasta and Chickpea Soup with Pesto

Preparation Time 25 minutes • Cooking Time about 1 hour • Serves 6 • Per Serving 211 calories, 8g fat (1g saturated), 26g carbohydrates, 300mg sodium • Easy

3 tablespoons olive oil

1 onion, chopped

2 garlic cloves, finely chopped

1 small leek, trimmed and sliced

1 teaspoon freshly chopped rosemary

1 (14-ounce) can chickpeas

4½ cups vegetable stock

4 ripe tomatoes, skinned and chopped

1 zucchini, diced

1 cup shelled peas

4 ounces green beans, halved

4 ounces shelled fava beans

½ cup dried pastina (small soup pasta)

2 tablespoons freshly chopped parsley

salt and ground black pepper

fresh ready-made pesto (see Cook's Tip) and freshly grated pecorino or Parmesan to serve

1. Heat the oil in a large pot, add the onion, garlic, leek, and rosemary and fry gently for 5–6 minutes or until softened but not colored. Add the chickpeas with their liquid, the stock, and tomatoes. Bring to a boil, and then reduce the heat, cover the pot, and simmer for 40 minutes.

2. Add the zucchini, peas, green beans, and fava beans. Return to a boil, and then reduce the heat, and simmer for 10 minutes. Add the pasta and parsley and simmer for 6–8 minutes until al dente. Season to taste with salt and pepper.

3. Ladle into warmed bowls and serve topped with a spoonful of pesto and a sprinkling of cheese.

COOK'S TIP

Fresh pesto

Put ¾ ounce roughly chopped basil into a food processor. Add ⅓ cup finely grated Parmesan, ½ cup pine nuts, and 4 tablespoons extra virgin olive oil and whiz to make a rough paste. Alternatively, grind with a mortar and pestle. Season with salt and plenty of ground black pepper.

Green Lentil and Coconut Soup

Preparation Time 20 minutes • Cooking Time 40 minutes • Serves 4 • Per Serving 442 calories, 22g fat (10g saturated), 48g carbohydrates, 300mg sodium • Vegetarian • Dairy Free • Easy

1⅓ cups whole green lentils
4 tablespoons sunflower oil
12 ounces baking potatoes, diced
1 large onion, chopped
2 garlic cloves, crushed
¼ teaspoon ground turmeric
2 teaspoons ground cumin
2 ounces creamed coconut

3 cups vegetable stock
1¼ cups coconut milk
finely grated zest of 1 lemon,
    plus extra to garnish
salt and ground black pepper
toasted fresh coconut (optional)
    to garnish

1. Put the lentils into a strainer and wash thoroughly under cold running water. Drain well.

2. Heat the oil in a large pot. Add the potatoes and fry gently for 5 minutes or until beginning to color. Remove with a slotted spoon and drain on paper towel.

3. Add the onion to the pot and fry gently for 10 minutes or until soft. Add the garlic, turmeric, and cumin and fry for 2–3 minutes. Add the coconut, stock, coconut milk, and lentils and bring to a boil. Reduce the heat, cover the pot, and simmer gently for 20 minutes or until the lentils are just tender.

4. Add the potatoes and lemon zest and season to taste with salt and pepper. Cook gently for another 5 minutes or until the potatoes are tender. Ladle into warmed bowls, garnish with toasted coconut and more lemon zest, if desired, and serve hot.

Simple Vegetable Soup

Preparation Time 15 minutes • Cooking Time 50 minutes • Serves 4 • Per Serving 96 calories,
6g fat (1g saturated), 8g carbohydrates, 200mg sodium • Vegetarian • Gluten Free • Dairy Free • Easy

1–2 onions, finely chopped

2 tablespoons olive oil or
   1 tablespoon olive oil and
   1 tablespoon butter

1–2 garlic cloves, crushed
   (optional)

1 pound mixed vegetables (such as
   leeks, potatoes, celery, fennel,
   tomatoes, and parsnips),
   chopped finely or cut into
   larger dice for a chunky soup

4²⁄₃ cups vegetable stock

1. Sauté the onions in the oil (or oil and butter) until soft and add the garlic, if desired.

2. Add the chopped mixed vegetables and the stock. Bring to a boil, and then reduce the heat and simmer for 20–30 minutes, until the vegetables are tender.

3. Leave chunky, partly puree, or blend until smooth.

Cauliflower Soup

Preparation Time 25 minutes • Cooking Time 40 minutes • Serves 6 • Per Serving 115 calories, 7g fat (1g saturated), 18g carbohydrates, 100mg sodium • Easy • Dairy free

3 cups coconut milk
3 cups vegetable stock
4 garlic cloves, finely chopped
2-inch piece fresh ginger, peeled
    and finely chopped
4 lemongrass stalks, coarsely
    chopped
4 red chilies, seeded and chopped
    (see Cook's Tip on page 15)
4 kaffir lime leaves, shredded
    (optional)
2 tablespoons peanut oil
2 teaspoons sesame oil
1 large onion, thinly sliced
2 teaspoons ground turmeric
2 teaspoons sugar
7 cups cauliflower florets
2 tablespoons lime juice
2 tablespoons light soy sauce
4 scallions, shredded
¼ cup freshly chopped cilantro
salt and ground black pepper

1. Put the coconut milk and stock into a large saucepan. Add the garlic and ginger with the lemongrass, chilies, and lime leaves. Bring to a boil, and then reduce the heat, cover the pan, and simmer for 15 minutes. Strain and keep the liquid to one side.

2. Heat the oils together in a clean saucepan. Add the onion, turmeric, and sugar, and sauté gently for 5 minutes. Add the cauliflower to the pan and stir-fry for 5 minutes or until lightly golden brown.

3. Add the reserved liquid, the lime juice, and soy sauce. Bring to a boil, and then reduce the heat, cover the pan, and simmer for 10–15 minutes, until the cauliflower is tender. Season with salt and black pepper. Divide among six warmed bowls. Sprinkle the scallions and cilantro on top and serve.

Pepper and Lentil Soup

Preparation Time 15 minutes • Cooking Time 45 minutes • Serves 6 • Per Serving 165 calories, 3g fat (1g saturated), 27g carbohydrates, 500mg sodium • Vegetarian • Dairy Free • Easy

1 tablespoon olive oil
1 medium onion, finely chopped
1 celery stick, chopped
1 leek, trimmed and chopped
1 carrot, chopped
**2 red bell peppers, seeded and
  diced**
1 cup red lentils
1 (14½-ounce) can diced tomatoes
4 cups hot light vegetable stock
**1 cup freshly chopped Italian
  parsley**
salt and ground black pepper
toast to serve

1. Heat the oil in a saucepan. Add the onion, celery, leek, and carrot and cook for 10–15 minutes, until soft.

2. Add the red bell peppers and cook for 5 minutes. Stir in the red lentils, add the tomatoes and hot stock, and season to taste with salt and black pepper.

3. Cover the pan and bring to a boil. Then reduce the heat and cook, uncovered, for 25 minutes or until the lentils are soft and the vegetables are tender.

4. Stir in the parsley. Ladle into warmed bowls and serve with toast.

Roasted Tomato and Pepper Soup

Preparation Time 20 minutes • Cooking Time about 1 hour • Serves 6 • Per Serving 239 calories,
16g fat (6g saturated), 15g carbohydrates, 400mg sodium • Gluten Free • Easy

12 ripe tomatoes (about 3 pounds)

2 red bell peppers, seeded and chopped

4 garlic cloves, crushed

3 small onions, thinly sliced

6 fresh thyme sprigs, plus extra leaves to garnish

¼ cup olive oil

3¼ cups boiling water

¼ cup Worcestershire sauce

¼ cup vodka*

salt and ground black pepper

⅓ cup heavy cream to serve

1. Preheat the oven to 400°F. Put the tomatoes in a large roasting pan with the red bell peppers, garlic, and onions. Scatter 6 thyme sprigs over the top, drizzle with the oil, and roast in the oven for 25 minutes. Turn the vegetables over and roast for another 30–40 minutes, until tender and slightly charred.

2. Put one-third of the vegetables into a blender or food processor with 1¼ cups of the boiling water. Add the Worcestershire sauce and vodka and season with salt and black pepper. Process until smooth, and then pass through a strainer into a saucepan.

3. Blend the remaining vegetables with the remaining boiling water. Then strain and add to the pan.

4. To serve, warm the soup thoroughly, stirring occasionally. Pour into warmed bowls, add 1 tablespoon heavy cream to each bowl, and drag a toothpick through the cream to swirl. Scatter a few fresh thyme leaves over the top and serve immediately.

* This recipe is not suitable for children because it contains alcohol.

Parsnip Soup with Chorizo

Preparation Time 20 minutes • Cooking Time 1 hour • Serves 8 • Per Serving 278 calories, 20g fat (9g saturated), 18g carbohydrates, 700mg sodium • Gluten Free • Easy

3 tablespoons butter

1 onion, coarsely chopped

2 red-skinned or white round potatoes, chopped

4 parsnips, chopped

4 teaspoons paprika, plus extra to dust

4½ cups vegetable stock

2 cups milk

¼ cup heavy cream

3 ounces sliced chorizo sausage, cut into fine strips

salt and ground black pepper

parsnip chips (optional) and freshly grated Parmesan to serve

1. Melt the butter in a large, heavy saucepan over gentle heat. Add the onion and cook for 5 minutes or until soft. Add the potatoes, parsnips, and paprika. Mix well and cook gently, stirring occasionally, for 15 minutes or until the vegetables begin to soften.

2. Add the stock, milk, and cream and season with salt and black pepper. Bring to a boil. Then reduce the heat and simmer for about 25 minutes or until the vegetables are soft. Add two-thirds of the chorizo. Let the soup cool a little, and then blend in a blender or food processor until smooth. The soup can be thinned with additional stock or milk, if desired. Check the seasoning and put back in the pan.

3. To serve, reheat the soup. Serve in warmed bowls and top each with parsnip chips, if desired. Sprinkle with the remaining chorizo and a little Parmesan, and dust with paprika.

FREEZING TIP

To freeze Complete the recipe to the end of step 2. Then cool, pack, and freeze for up to one month.
To use Thaw the soup overnight at cool room temperature, and then complete the recipe.

French Onion Soup

Preparation Time 30 minutes • Cooking Time about 1 hour • Serves 4 • Per Serving 438 calories, 21g fat (13g saturated), 45g carbohydrates, 1,300mg sodium • Vegetarian • Easy

6 tablespoons butter

10 small onions (about 1½ pounds), finely chopped

3 garlic cloves, crushed

1 tablespoon all-purpose flour

¾ cup dry white wine* (optional)

6 cups vegetable stock

1 bouquet garni (see Cook's Tip on page 19)

salt and ground black pepper

TO SERVE

1 small loaf French bread, cut into slices ½ inch thick

½ cup shredded Gruyère or cheddar cheese (see Cook's Tip on page 130)

1. Melt the butter in a large, heavy saucepan. Add the onions and cook slowly over low heat, stirring frequently, until soft and golden brown; this should take at least 30 minutes. Add the garlic and flour and cook, stirring, for 1 minute.

2. Pour in the wine, if using, and simmer until reduced by half. Add the stock, bouquet garni, and seasoning. Bring to a boil, and then reduce the heat and simmer gently, uncovered, for 20–30 minutes.

3. Discard the bouquet garni and let the soup cool a little. Process one-third in a food processor or blender until smooth, then stir this back into the soup in the pan.

4. Preheat the broiler. Lightly toast the bread slices on both sides. Reheat the onion soup and adjust the seasoning.

5. Divide the soup among four ovenproof soup bowls. Float two or three slices of toast on each portion and sprinkle thickly with the shredded cheese. Stand the bowls under the hot broiler until the cheese has melted and turned golden brown. Serve at once.

* This recipe is not suitable for children if it contains alcohol.

Hearty Chicken Soup with Dumplings

Preparation Time 20 minutes • Cooking Time 40 minutes • Serves 4 • Per Serving 335 calories,
15g fat (5g saturated), 31g carbohydrates, 300mg sodium • Easy

2 tablespoons olive oil

2 celery sticks, coarsely chopped

3 small carrots, coarsely chopped

5 ounces new potatoes, thinly
sliced

10 ounces boneless, skinless
chicken breast, thinly sliced

8½ cups hot chicken stock

⅔ cup frozen peas

salt and ground black pepper

a handful of coarsely chopped
chives, to garnish (optional)

FOR THE DUMPLINGS

¾ cup all-purpose flour

½ teaspoon baking powder

½ teaspoon salt

1 large egg, well beaten

2 tablespoons butter, melted

a splash of milk

1. Heat the oil in a large saucepan, and then add the celery, carrots, and potatoes. Cook for 5 minutes or until the vegetables begin to caramelize around the edges. Add the chicken and cook for 3 minutes or until just starting to brown. Pour in the hot stock and simmer for 15 minutes, skimming the surface occasionally to remove any scum.

2. To make the dumplings, sift the flour, baking powder, and salt into a bowl, then season with black pepper. Combine the egg, melted butter, and milk in a separate bowl. Then stir quickly into the flour to make a stiff batter.

3. Drop half teaspoonfuls of the dumpling mixture into the soup. Cover and simmer for another 15 minutes.

4. Stir in the peas and heat through. Check the seasoning, sprinkle with black pepper, and serve garnished with chives, if desired.

Turkey and Chestnut Soup

Preparation Time 5 minutes • Cooking Time 45 minutes • Serves 4 • Per Serving 330 calories,
10g fat (5g saturated), 52g carbohydrates, 200mg sodium • Gluten Free • Easy

2 tablespoons butter or margarine
1 large onion, chopped
8 ounces brussels sprouts
3½ cups turkey stock
**1½ (10-ounce) cans whole
    chestnuts, drained**

**2 teaspoons freshly chopped thyme
    or 1 teaspoon dried thyme**
salt and ground black pepper
stock or milk to finish
thyme sprigs to garnish

1. Melt the fat in a large, heavy saucepan, add the onion, and cook gently for 5 minutes or until the onion has softened.

2. Trim the sprouts and cut a cross in the bottom of each one. Add to the onion, cover the pan with a lid, and cook gently for 5 minutes, shaking the pan frequently.

3. Pour in the stock and bring to a boil. Add the remaining ingredients, with salt and black pepper to taste. Reduce the heat, cover the pan, and simmer for 30 minutes or until the vegetables are tender.

4. Let the soup cool a little. Blend in batches in a blender or food processor until smooth. Return to the rinsed-out pan and reheat gently. Thin down with either stock or milk, according to taste.

5. Taste and adjust the seasoning. To serve, ladle into warmed bowls and garnish with sprigs of thyme.

COOK'S TIP
For an informal family lunch, serve with hot garlic bread, dinner rolls, or wheat toast.

Hot and Sour Soup

Preparation Time 20 minutes • Cooking Time 30–35 minutes • Serves 4 • Per Serving 255 calories, 10g fat (1g saturated), 19g carbohydrates, 700mg sodium • Dairy Free • Easy

1 tablespoon vegetable oil

2 turkey cutlets, about 11 ounces, or the same quantity of tofu, cut into strips

2-inch piece fresh ginger, peeled and grated

4 scallions, finely sliced

1–2 tablespoons Thai red curry paste

⅓ cup long-grain wild rice

4½ cups hot, weak chicken or vegetable stock or boiling water

3 cups sliced snow peas

juice of 1 lime

¼ cup coarsely chopped fresh cilantro to garnish

1. Heat the oil in a saucepan. Add the turkey or tofu and cook over medium heat for 5 minutes or until browned. Add the ginger and scallions and cook for another 2–3 minutes. Stir in the curry paste and cook for 1–2 minutes to warm the spices.

2. Add the rice and stir to coat in the curry paste. Pour the hot stock or boiling water into the pan, stir once, and bring to a boil. Reduce the heat, cover the pan, and simmer for 20 minutes.

3. Add the snow peas and cook for another 5 minutes or until the rice is cooked. Just before serving, squeeze in the lime juice and stir.

4. To serve, ladle into warmed bowls and sprinkle with the cilantro.

FISH AND SHELLFISH

Roasted Salmon

Preparation Time 20 minutes, plus cooling and chilling • Cooking Time about 30 minutes • Serves 20 •
Per Serving 347 calories, 25g fat (9g saturated), 3g carbohydrates, 200mg sodium • Gluten Free • Easy

3 lemons, 2 sliced and the juice
   of ½, plus extra lemon slices
   to garnish
2 (3-pound) salmon fillets, with
   skin on, boned and trimmed
2 tablespoons dry white wine*
salt and ground black pepper
cucumber slices and 2 large
   bunches of watercress to garnish

FOR THE DRESSING

2 cups crème fraîche
2 cups plain yogurt
2 tablespoons horseradish sauce
3 tablespoons freshly chopped
   tarragon
¼ cup capers, coarsely chopped,
   plus extra to garnish
¼ cucumber, halved lengthwise,
   seeded and finely chopped,
   to garnish

1. Preheat the oven to 375°F. Take two pieces of aluminum foil, each large enough to wrap one side of salmon, and put a piece of parchment paper on top of each foil. Divide the lemon slices between each piece of parchment paper and lay the salmon on top, skin side up. Season with salt and black pepper, and pour the lemon juice and wine over the fish.

2. Score the skin of each salmon fillet at 1½-inch intervals to mark 10 portions. Scrunch the foil around each fillet, keeping it uncovered and loose so that the fish doesn't stick. Place the wrapped fillets on a baking sheet and cook for 25 minutes or until the flesh is just opaque. Unwrap the foil and cook for another 5 minutes, until the skin is crisp. Let the fish cool quickly in a cold place. Rewrap and chill.

3. Put all the dressing ingredients, except the garnishes, in a bowl and season with salt and black pepper. Mix well, cover, and chill.

4. Serve the salmon on a platter garnished with lemon, cucumber, and watercress. Garnish the dressing with capers and chopped cucumber and serve on the side.

* This recipe is not suitable for children because it contains alcohol.

COOK'S TIPS

• *There'll be a lot of hot liquid in the package of salmon, so be careful when removing it from the oven.*
• *To check the fish is cooked, ease a knife into one of the slashes in the skin. The flesh should look opaque and the knife should come out hot.*
• *If you want to prepare this in advance, complete the recipe to the end of step 3, then keep the salmon wrapped and chilled for up to one day.*

Salmon and Asparagus Pie

Preparation time 40 minutes, plus chilling and cooling • Cooking time 1 hour 10 minutes • Serves 6 •
Per serving 782 calories, 59g fat (32g saturated), 37g carbohydrates, 800mg sodium • A Little Effort

2½ cups all-purpose flour, plus
    extra to dust
¾ cup plus 2 tablespoons
    (1¾ sticks) chilled butter, cubed
1 extra-large egg, beaten, plus
    1 extra-large egg, beaten,
    to glaze
2 tablespoons cold water

FOR THE FILLING

2 extra-large eggs and 2 extra-large
    yolks, beaten
1 cup crème fraîche
3 tablespoons freshly chopped dill
2 tablespoons butter

3 cups white mushrooms, sliced
¾ cup thick asparagus tips
1 pound skinless salmon fillet, cut
    into wide strips, 4½ inch long
salt and ground black pepper

1. Process the flour, butter, and salt in a food processor until they resemble bread crumbs. Add one egg and the cold water and pulse until the mixture just comes together. Knead lightly. Cut off one-third, wrap both pieces, and chill for 30 minutes.

2. Preheat the oven to 400°F. Roll out the larger piece of dough to a 11-inch round. Use to line an 8-inch wide, 2-inch deep, loose-based pie pan and prick the bottom with a fork. Line with parchment paper and pie weights and put on a baking sheet. Bake for 25 minutes. Remove the paper and weights, brush the pastry with beaten egg, and cook for 5–10 minutes until the pie shell is almost cooked. Cool.

3. To make the filling, combine the whole eggs, crème fraîche, and dill and season. Melt the butter and fry the mushrooms for 1–2 minutes. Season and cool. Add the asparagus to boiling water, return to a boil, and then drain. Refresh in iced water. Arrange half the fish in the pie shell. Arrange the vegetables on top. Finish with the remaining fish and pour the crème fraîche mixture over to within ½ inch of the top. Brush the edge with beaten egg. Cut the remaining dough into a 10-inch round, place on top and seal the edges. Brush with egg and make a steam hole. Put the baking sheet in the oven to heat. Bake the pie on the tray for 40 minutes or until golden and the filling is cooked. Cool in the pan.

COOK'S TIPS

• *To check the pie is cooked, insert a skewer into the center for 30 seconds—it should feel hot when you pull it out.*

• *Cool the pie in the pan for 1 hour to serve warm, or 3 hours to serve at room temperature.*

Luxury Smoked Fish Casserole

Preparation Time 30 minutes • Cooking Time 1 hour 20 minutes • Serves 4 • Per Serving 1057 calories, 63g fat (34g saturated), 66g carbohydrates, 3,800mg sodium • Easy

10 red-skinned or white round potatoes (about 2½ pounds) peeled and cut into chunks
2 cups milk
½ cup (1 stick) butter
1 cup shredded cheddar cheese
⅓ cup dry white wine*
⅔ cup fish stock
1 pound skinless smoked haddock fillet or other smoked fish, cut into wide strips
12 ounces skinless salmon fillet, cut into wide strips
¼ cup all-purpose flour
⅓ cup heavy cream
1 tablespoon capers, drained, rinsed, and chopped
1½ tablespoons freshly chopped Italian parsley
2 large eggs, hard-cooked
salt and ground black pepper

1. Preheat the oven to 350°F. Put the potatoes into a saucepan of lightly salted water and bring to a boil. Cover the pan, reduce the heat, and simmer until tender.

2. Warm ½ cup milk. Drain the potatoes, then put back into the pan over low heat for 2 minutes. Mash until smooth. Stir in 5 tablespoons butter, half the cheese, and the warmed milk, then season with salt and black pepper. Cover and put to one side.

3. Meanwhile, bring the wine, stock, and remaining milk to a boil in a large, wide saucepan. Add the haddock and salmon and return the liquid to a boil. Reduce the heat to poach the fish gently for 5 minutes or until it flakes easily. Lift the fish with a draining spoon into a 1½-quart, deep ovenproof dish and flake with a fork, if necessary. Put the cooking liquid to one side.

4. Melt the remaining butter in another saucepan, add the flour, and stir until smooth. Cook for 2 minutes. Gradually add the fish cooking liquid, whisking until smooth. Bring to a boil, stirring, and cook for 2 minutes or until thickened. Stir in the cream, capers, and parsley and season to taste with salt and black pepper.

5. Shell the eggs and coarsely chop. Sprinkle over the fish, and then pour over the sauce. Spoon the potato mixture on top. Sprinkle with the remaining cheese.

6. Bake the casserole for 35–40 minutes until golden brown and bubbling at the edges. Serve hot.

* This recipe is not suitable for children because it contains alcohol.

Herby Lemon Fishcakes

Preparation Time 25 minutes, plus cooling • Cooking Time about 45 minutes • Serves 4 • Per Serving 721 calories, 42g fat (7g saturated), 37g carbohydrates, 500mg sodium • Gluten Free • Dairy Free • Easy

8 russet or Yukon gold potatoes
   (about 2 pounds), peeled and
   quartered
2 pounds skinless salmon fillets
2½ cups cold water
juice of 1 lemon
¼ cup mayonnaise
a pinch of cayenne pepper
2 tablespoons freshly chopped
   herbs (such as tarragon, basil,
   or parsley), plus extra leaves
   to garnish
2 tablespoons chili oil
salt and ground black pepper
lemon wedges to garnish
green salad to serve

1. Put the potatoes into a large saucepan of lightly salted cold water, cover, and bring to a boil. Reduce the heat and simmer for 20 minutes or until tender. Drain well, put the pan back on the heat to dry the potatoes, then mash.

2. Meanwhile, put the salmon into a saucepan with the cold water and half the lemon juice. Cover and bring to a boil. Then reduce the heat and simmer for 1 minute. Turn off the heat and let cool in the water for 20–30 minutes.

3. Preheat the oven to 400°F. Drain the fish, remove the skin and discard, and then flake the fish. Add to the potato along with the remaining lemon juice, the mayonnaise, cayenne pepper, and chopped herbs. Season and mix together.

4. Line a large baking sheet with aluminum foil. Put a 3-inch plain cooking ring on the baking sheet and fill with some of the mixture. Lift off, and then repeat with the remainder of the mixture to make eight cakes. Drizzle with chili oil and bake for 25 minutes or until golden brown. Garnish with herbs and lemon wedges, and serve with a green salad.

COOK'S TIP
If your fishcakes tend to fall apart, put them in the refrigerator for about 2 hours (or 30 minutes in the freezer) before cooking them.

Spanish Fish Stew

Preparation Time 20 minutes • Cooking Time 1 hour 10 minutes • Serves 4 • Per Serving 463 calories, 22g fat (6g saturated), 32g carbohydrates, 1,800mg sodium • Gluten Free • Dairy Free • Easy

12 ounces small new potatoes, halved
6 ounces chorizo sausage, skinned and coarsely chopped
1 (12-ounce) jar roasted peppers in olive oil, drained and chopped, oil reserved
1 garlic clove, crushed
2 small red onions, cut into thick wedges
¾ cup dry white wine*
1¼ cups canned tomato puree or tomato sauce
2 tablespoons ripe black olives, pitted
1 pound chunky white fish (such as cod and halibut), cut into large cubes
salt and ground black pepper
freshly chopped Italian parsley to garnish

1. Preheat the oven to 340°F. Put the potatoes, chorizo, roasted peppers, garlic, onions, wine, and canned tomato puree or sauce into a large flameproof Dutch oven with 2 tablespoons of the oil from the roasted peppers. Season with salt and black pepper.

2. Bring to a boil over medium heat. Cover with a tight-fitting lid and bake in the oven for 45 minutes.

3. Add the olives and fish and put back in the oven for 15 minutes or until the fish is opaque and completely cooked through. Spoon into warmed bowls, garnish with chopped parsley and serve.

* This recipe is not suitable for children because it contains alcohol.

Scallops with Ginger

Preparation Time 15 minutes • Cooking Time 3 minutes • Serves 4 • Per Serving 197 calories, 7g fat (1g saturated), 6g carbohydrates, 2,000mg sodium • Dairy Free • Easy

2 tablespoons vegetable oil

1 pound shelled large scallops, cut into ¼-inch slices

4 celery sticks, sliced diagonally

1 bunch of scallions, sliced diagonally

¼-inch piece fresh ginger, peeled and sliced

2 large garlic cloves, sliced

¼ teaspoon chili powder

2 tablespoons lemon juice

2 tablespoons light soy sauce

3 tablespoons freshly chopped cilantro

salt and ground black pepper

1. Heat the oil in a wok or large skillet. Add the scallops, celery, scallions, ginger, garlic, and chili powder and stir-fry over high heat for 2 minutes or until the vegetables are just tender.

2. Pour in the lemon juice and soy sauce and bring to a simmer. Stir in about 2 tablespoons chopped cilantro and season with salt and black pepper. Serve immediately, sprinkled with the remaining cilantro.

Mussels with White Wine

Preparation Time 15 minutes • Cooking Time 20 minutes • Serves 4 • Per Serving 266 calories, 13g fat (7g saturated), 2g carbohydrates, 900mg sodium • Gluten Free • Easy

4½ pounds fresh mussels, scrubbed, rinsed and beards removed (see Cook's Tip)
2 tablespoons butter
4 shallots, finely chopped
2 garlic cloves, crushed
¾ cup dry white wine*
2 tablespoons freshly chopped Italian parsley
½ cup light cream
salt and ground black pepper
crusty bread to serve

1. Tap the mussels on the work surface and discard any that do not close or have broken shells. Heat the butter in a large nonstick lidded skillet and sauté the shallots over medium-high heat for about 10 minutes or until soft.

2. Add the garlic, wine, and half the parsley to the skillet and bring to a boil. Add the mussels and reduce the heat a little. Cover and cook for about 5 minutes or until all the shells have opened; discard any mussels that don't open.

3. Lift out the mussels with a slotted spoon and put into serving bowls. Cover with aluminum foil to keep warm. Add the cream to the stock, season with salt and black pepper, and cook for 1–2 minutes to heat through.

4. Pour a little sauce over the mussels and sprinkle with the rest of the parsley. Serve immediately with crusty bread.

* This recipe is not suitable for children because it contains alcohol.

COOK'S TIP
To prepare mussels, scrape off the fibers attached to the shells (beards). If the mussels are clean, give them a quick rinse under running cold water. If they are sandy, scrub them with a stiff brush. If the shells have sizable barnacles on them, it's best (though not essential) to remove them. Tap them sharply with a metal spoon on the back and then scrape off the barnacles. Discard any open mussels that don't shut when tapped sharply; this means they are dead and could be dangerous to eat.

Crab Cakes

Preparation Time 15 minutes • Cooking Time 6 minutes • Serves 4 • Per Serving 124 calories, 4g fat (1g saturated), 12g carbohydrates, 900mg sodium • Gluten Free • Dairy Free • Easy

7 ounces fresh crabmeat

2 scallions, finely chopped

2 red chilies, seeded and finely chopped (see Cook's Tip on page 15)

finely grated zest of 1 lime

¼ cup freshly chopped cilantro

¾ cup whole-wheat bread crumbs

1 tablespoon peanut oil

1 tablespoon all-purpose flour

1 red chili, thinly sliced, to garnish

1 lime, cut into wedges, and salad greens to serve

1. Put the crabmeat into a bowl, then add the scallions, chilies, lime zest, and cilantro and stir to mix. Add enough bread crumbs to hold the mixture together, and form into four small patties.

2. Heat ½ tablespoon oil in a saucepan. Dredge the patties with flour and cook on one side for 3 minutes. Add the rest of the oil, turn the patties over, and cook for another 2–3 minutes. Garnish the crab cakes with thinly sliced red chilies; serve with lime wedges to squeeze over them, and salad greens.

Smoked Haddock and Potato Pie

Preparation Time 15 minutes • Cooking Time 1¼ hours–1 hour 25 minutes • Serves 4 • Per Serving 380 calories, 20g fat (11g saturated), 37g carbohydrates, 1,500mg sodium • Gluten Free • Easy

½ cup heavy cream
⅔ cup fish stock
3 medium russet potatoes, thinly sliced
12 ounces skinless smoked haddock fillets, coarsely chopped
½ cup freshly chopped chives
1 large onion, finely chopped
salt and ground black pepper
green salad to serve

1. Preheat the oven to 400°F. Pour the cream into a large bowl. Add the fish stock and stir well to combine.

2. Add the potatoes, haddock, chives, and onion and season with salt and black pepper. Toss everything together to coat. Spoon the mixture into a shallow 2½-quart ovenproof dish.

3. Cover the dish with aluminum foil, put it on a baking sheet, and bake for 45 minutes. Remove the foil and bake for another 30–40 minutes until bubbling and the top is golden brown.

4. To check that the potatoes are cooked, insert the tip of a sharp knife—it should push in easily. If you desire, put the dish under a hot broiler to make the top layer crisp. Let cool slightly. Serve with a green salad.

COOK'S TIP
For the lightest texture, make sure you use large, floury potatoes. New potatoes are too waxy.

CHICKEN
DISHES

One-Pot Chicken

Preparation Time 20 minutes • Cooking Time 1 hour 40 minutes • Serves 6 • Per Serving 474 calories, 33g fat (9g saturated), 6g carbohydrates, 600mg sodium • Dairy Free • Easy

2 tablespoons olive oil
1 large onion, cut into wedges
2 slices bacon, chopped
1 chicken, about 3½ pounds
6 carrots
2 small turnips, cut into wedges
1 garlic clove, crushed
1 bouquet garni (see Cook's Tip on
   page 19)
2½ cups hot chicken stock
½ cup dry white wine*
12 white mushrooms
3 tablespoon freshly chopped
   Italian parsley
salt and ground black pepper
mashed potatoes to serve (optional)

1. Heat the oil in a nonstick Dutch oven. Add the onion and bacon and sauté for 5 minutes or until golden brown. Remove the onion and bacon and set aside.

2. Add the whole chicken to the same Dutch oven and cook for 10 minutes, turning carefully to brown all over. Remove the chicken and set aside.

3. Preheat the oven to 400°F. Add the carrots, turnips, and garlic to the pot. Sauté for 5 minutes, and then add the bacon and onion. Put the chicken back into the pot, add the bouquet garni, hot stock, and wine and season with salt and black pepper. Bring to a simmer. Then cover the pot and roast in the oven for 30 minutes.

4. Remove the pot from the oven and add the mushrooms. Baste the chicken. Replace the lid and roast for another 50 minutes.

5. Lift out the chicken, and then stir the parsley into the cooking liquid. Carve the chicken and serve with the vegetables, cooking liquid, and mashed potatoes, if desired.

* This recipe is not suitable for children because it contains alcohol.

TRY SOMETHING DIFFERENT
Using chicken pieces such as drumsticks or thighs reduces the cooking time in step 4 to 20 minutes.

Tarragon Chicken with Fennel

Preparation Time 10 minutes • Cooking Time 45–55 minutes • Serves 4 • Per Serving 334 calories, 26g fat (15g saturated), 3g carbohydrates, 500mg sodium • Easy

1 tablespoon olive oil
4 chicken thighs
1 onion, finely chopped
1 fennel bulb, finely chopped
juice of ½ lemon
¾ cup hot chicken stock
¾ cup crème fraîche or heavy cream
a small bunch of tarragon, coarsely chopped
salt and ground black pepper

1. Preheat the oven to 400°F. Heat the oil in a large Dutch oven over medium high heat. Add the chicken thighs and sauté for 5 minutes or until browned. Remove and put them to one side to keep warm.

2. Add the onion to the pot and sauté for 5 minutes. Then add the fennel and cook for 5–10 minutes until softened.

3. Add the lemon juice to the pot, followed by the hot stock. Bring to a simmer and cook until the sauce is reduced by half.

4. Stir in the crème fraîche or cream and put the chicken back into the pot. Stir once to mix. Cover and bake in the oven for 25–30 minutes. Stir the tarragon into the sauce, season with salt and black pepper, and serve.

Oven-Baked Chicken with Garlic Potatoes

Preparation Time 10 minutes • Cooking Time 1½ hours • Serves 6 • Per Serving 376 calories, 16g fat (5g saturated), 32g carbohydrates, 1,200mg sodium • Easy

2 medium russet potatoes, thinly sliced

a little freshly grated nutmeg

2½ cups white sauce (use a store-bought sauce or make your own, see Cook's Tip)

2 cups cooked onions, thawed if frozen, diced or sliced

2½ cups frozen peas

1 pound cooked chicken, shredded

1½ tablespoons garlic butter, sliced

a little butter to grease

salt and ground black pepper

whole-grain bread to serve (optional)

1. Preheat the oven to 350°F. Layer half the potatoes over the bottom of a shallow 2-quart ovenproof dish and season with the nutmeg, salt, and black pepper. Pour the white sauce over the top and shake the dish, so that the sauce settles through the gaps in the potatoes.

2. Spread half the onions on top, and then sprinkle with half the peas. Arrange the shredded chicken on top. Add the remaining peas and onions.

3. Finish with the remaining potatoes, arranged in an even layer, and dot with garlic butter. Season with salt and black pepper.

4. Cover tightly with buttered aluminum foil and bake for 1 hour. Turn up the heat to 400°F, remove the foil, and continue to bake for 20–30 minutes, until the potatoes are golden and tender. Serve with whole-grain bread, if desired, to mop up the juices.

COOK'S TIP
White Sauce
To make 2½ cups white sauce, melt 2 tablespoons butter in a saucepan, and then stir in ¼ cup all-purpose flour. Cook, stirring constantly, for 1 minute. Remove from the heat and gradually pour in 2½ cups milk, beating after each addition. Return to the heat and cook, stirring, until the sauce has thickened and is velvety and smooth. Season with salt, black pepper, and freshly grated nutmeg. To make a cheesy white sauce, add 1–2 cups grated cheddar cheese and replace the nutmeg with a pinch of cayenne powder.

Chicken with Green Olives and Lemons

Preparation Time 15 minutes • Cooking Time about 1 hour 20 minutes • Serves 6 • Per Serving 347 calories, 22g fat (5g saturated), 7g carbohydrates, 900mg sodium • Dairy Free • Easy

½ teaspoon each ground turmeric, ginger, and coriander
1½ tablespoons all-purpose flour
6 chicken legs, with skin on
2 tablespoons olive oil
1 medium onion, coarsely chopped
1 garlic clove, thinly sliced
½ cup manzanilla or fino sherry*
3½ cups hot chicken stock
3 preserved lemons
½ cup green olives, pitted and sliced
juice of ½ lemon
salt and ground black pepper

1. Put the spices and flour into a plastic sandwich bag and season. Add the chicken and shake until covered with the flour mixture. Shake off the excess and set aside any leftover flour.

2. Heat 1 tablespoon oil in a large Dutch oven over medium heat. Sauté the chicken in batches until golden bown. Avoid overcrowding the pot, because it will lower the temperature and the chicken will not brown. Remove the chicken and set aside.

3. Put the remaining oil in the same pot and cook the onion over low heat for 10 minutes. Add the garlic and cook for 1 minute. Turn up the heat to medium and add the leftover flour. Cook for 1 minute, stirring to soak up the oil. Scrape up any browned sediment from the bottom of the pot—this will add flavor. Gradually stir in the sherry (it will bubble and thicken), followed by the hot stock.

4. Halve the lemons, scrape out the pulp and discard. Add the peel to the pot along with the chicken. Cover the pot and simmer over low heat for 30 minutes. Stir in the olives and cook for 15 minutes or until the chicken is done—the juices should run clear when you pierce the flesh with the tip of a sharp knife.

5. Remove the chicken, olives, onions, and lemons with a slotted spoon (don't worry if you leave some onion behind) and keep them warm. Turn up the heat and boil the sauce rapidly until it reduces by about one-third and turns syrupy. Taste and add more seasoning, if it needs it, along with the lemon juice.

6. Return the chicken, olives, onion, and lemons to the pot and serve.

This recipe is not suitable for children because it contains alcohol.

COOK'S TIP
If you have leftover preserved lemons, the next time you roast a whole chicken put a couple inside the bird along with a few fresh thyme sprigs.

Herb Chicken with Roasted Vegetables

Preparation Time 15 minutes, plus marinating • Cooking Time 40 minutes • Serves 4 • Per Serving 453 calories, 29g fat (7g saturated), 10g carbohydrates, 300mg sodium • Gluten Free • Dairy Free • Easy

2 garlic cloves
1 cup fresh basil
1 cup fresh mint
8 fresh lemon thyme sprigs
¼ cup olive oil
4 whole chicken legs (drumsticks and thighs)
1 small eggplant, chopped
12 baby plum tomatoes
2 red bell peppers, seeded and chopped
2 zucchini, sliced
juice of 1 lemon
salt and ground black pepper
green salad to serve

1. Put the garlic, two-thirds of the basil and mint, and the leaves from 4 lemon thyme sprigs into a food processor and process, gradually adding half the oil until the mixture forms a thick paste. (Alternatively, use a mortar and pestle.)

2. Rub the paste over the chicken legs, then put into a bowl. Cover, then chill and let marinate for at least 30 minutes.

3. Preheat the oven to 400°F. Put the eggplant, plum tomatoes, red bell peppers, and zucchini in a large roasting pan with the remaining oil and season with salt and black pepper. Toss to coat. Add the chicken and roast for 30–40 minutes, until the vegetables are tender and the chicken cooked through.

4. Squeeze the lemon juice over the chicken and stir in the remaining herbs. Serve immediately with a crisp green salad.

Jambalaya

Preparation Time 15 minutes • Cooking Time about 50 minutes, plus standing • Serves 4 • Per Serving 558 calories, 25g fat (6g saturated), 49g carbohydrates, 0mg sodium • Gluten Free • Dairy Free • Easy

2 tablespoons olive oil
12 ounces boneless, skinless chicken thighs, cut into chunks
3 ounces French sausage (such as saucisse sèche, or other good-quality link sausage), chopped
2 celery sticks, chopped
1 large onion, finely chopped
1 cup long-grain rice
1 tablespoon tomato paste
2 teaspoons Cajun spice mix
2 cups hot chicken stock
1 bay leaf
4 large tomatoes, coarsely chopped
8 ounces jumbo shrimp, peeled and deveined (see Cook's Tip)

1. Heat 1 tablespoon oil in a large saucepan and cook the chicken and sausage over medium heat until browned. Remove with a slotted spoon and set aside.

2. Add the remaining oil to the pan with the celery and onion. Sauté gently for 15 minutes or until the vegetables are softened but not browned. Add the rice and stir for 1 minute to coat in the oil. Add the tomato paste and spice mix and cook for another 2 minutes.

3. Pour in the hot stock and return the browned chicken and sausage to the pan with the bay leaf and tomatoes. Simmer for 20–25 minutes, until the stock has been fully absorbed and the rice is cooked.

4. Stir in the shrimp and cover the pan. Let stand for 10 minutes or until the shrimp have turned pink. Serve immediately.

COOK'S TIP

To devein shrimp, pull off the head and discard (or put to one side and use later for making stock). Using pointed scissors, cut through the soft shell on the belly side. Peel off the shell, leaving the tail attached. (The shell can also be used later for making stock.) Using a small sharp knife, make a shallow cut along the back of the shrimp. Using the point of the knife, remove and discard the black vein (the intestinal tract) that runs along the back of the shrimp.

Spiced Chicken Pilaf

Preparation Time 15 minutes • Cooking Time 35–40 minutes • Serves 4 • Per Serving 649 calories, 18g fat (2g saturated), 87g carbohydrates, 2,800mg sodium • Dairy Free • Easy

⅓ cup pine nuts

2 tablespoons olive oil

2 onions, sliced

2 garlic cloves, crushed

2 tablespoons medium curry powder

6 boneless, skinless chicken thighs or 1 pound skinless cooked chicken, cut into strips

1¾ cups long-grain rice

3½ cups boiling water

2 teaspoons salt

a pinch of saffron threads

¼ cup golden raisins

2 ripe tomatoes, coarsely chopped

1. Spread the pine nuts over a baking sheet and toast under a hot broiler until golden brown, turning them frequently. Put to one side.

2. Heat the oil in a large, heavy saucepan over medium heat. Add the onions and garlic and cook for 5 minutes or until soft. Remove half the onion mixture and put to one side.

3. Add the curry powder and cook for 1 minute, and then add the chicken and stir. Cook for 10 minutes if the meat is raw, or for 4 minutes if you're using cooked chicken, stirring from time to time until browned.

4. Add the rice to the pan and stir to coat in the oil. Then add the boiling water, the salt, and saffron. Cover the pan and bring to a boil. Reduce the heat to low and cook for 20 minutes or until the rice is tender and most of the liquid has been absorbed. Stir in the reserved onion mixture and the golden raisins, tomatoes, and pine nuts. Cook for another 5 minutes to warm through, then serve.

COOK'S TIP

This is a good way to use up leftover roast turkey.

Moroccan Chicken with Chickpeas

Preparation Time 10 minutes • Cooking Time 50 minutes • Serves 6 • Per Serving 440 calories, 18g fat (6g saturated), 33g carbohydrates, 1,000mg sodium • Easy

12 chicken pieces, such as thighs, drumsticks, and breasts

2 tablespoons butter

1 large onion, sliced

2 garlic cloves, crushed

2 tablespoons harissa paste

a generous pinch of saffron threads

1 teaspoon salt

1 cinnamon stick

2½ cups chicken stock

½ cup raisins

2 (15-ounce) cans chickpeas, drained and rinsed

ground black pepper

plain naan or pita bread to serve

1. Heat a large, wide nonstick saucepan. Add the chicken pieces and cook until well browned all over. Add the butter and, when melted, add the onion and garlic. Cook, stirring, for 5 minutes.

2. Add the harissa, saffron, salt, and cinnamon stick, then season well with black pepper. Pour in the stock and bring to a boil. Reduce the heat, cover the pan, and simmer gently for 25–30 minutes.

3. Add the raisins and chickpeas and bring to a boil. Reduce the heat and simmer uncovered for 5–10 minutes.

4. Serve with warm flatbread such as plain naan or pita.

FREEZING TIP

To freeze *Freeze leftover portions separately. Complete the recipe, then cool quickly. Put into a sealable container and freeze for up to 3 months.*

To use *Thaw overnight in the refrigerator. Put into a saucepan, cover, and bring to a boil. Reduce the heat to low, then reheat for 40 minutes or until the chicken is hot right through.*

Caribbean Chicken

Preparation Time 40 minutes, plus marinating • Cooking Time 45–50 minutes • Serves 5 • Per Serving 617 calories, 39g fat (12g saturated), 25g carbohydrates, 2,100mg sodium • Easy

10 chicken pieces (such as thighs, drumsticks, wings, or breasts), skinned

1 teaspoon salt

1 tablespoon ground coriander

2 teaspoons ground cumin

1 tablespoon paprika

a pinch of ground nutmeg

1 fresh Scotch bonnet pepper or other hot red chili, seeded and chopped (see page 15)

1 onion, chopped

5 fresh thyme sprig, plus extra to garnish

4 garlic cloves, crushed

2 tablespoons dark soy sauce

juice of 1 lemon

2 tablespoons vegetable oil

2 tablespoons packed light brown sugar

1¾ cups long-grain rice

3½ cups cold water

3 tablespoons dark rum* (optional)

2 tablespoons butter

2½ cups canned black-eyed peas, drained and rinsed

ground black pepper

1. Pierce the chicken pieces with a knife, put into a container, and sprinkle with ½ teaspoon salt, some black pepper, the coriander, cumin, paprika, and nutmeg. Add the chili, onion, thyme leaves, and garlic. Pour the soy sauce and lemon juice over the meat and stir to combine. Cover and chill for at least 4 hours.

2. Heat a 3-quart heavy saucepan over medium heat for 2 minutes. Add the oil and sugar and cook for 3 minutes or until it turns a golden caramel color. (Don't overcook it because the mixture will blacken and taste burned; watch it closely.) Remove the chicken from the marinade. Add to the caramel mixture. Cover and cook over medium heat for 5 minutes. Turn the chicken and cook, covered, for another 5 minutes or until evenly browned. Add the onion mixture and any marinade juices. Turn again, then replace the lid and cook for 10 minutes.

3. Add the rice and stir to combine with the chicken, and then pour in the cold water. Add the rum, if using, the butter, and the remaining salt. Cover and simmer over gentle heat, without lifting the lid, for 20 minutes or until the rice is tender and most of the liquid has been absorbed.

4. Add the black-eyed peas to the pan and mix well. Cover the pan and cook for 3–5 minutes, until the beans are warmed through and all the liquid has been absorbed, being careful that the rice doesn't stick to the bottom of the pan. Garnish with the thyme sprigs and serve hot.

* This recipe is not suitable for children if it contains alcohol.

Chicken Curry

Preparation Time 20–25 minutes • Cooking Time about 50 minutes • Serves 4 • Per Serving 342 calories, 10g fat (2g saturated), 25g carbohydrates, 500mg sodium • Gluten Free • Dairy Free • Easy

1 tablespoon olive oil
4 chicken legs, skinned
1 onion, finely chopped
2 tablespoons mild or medium
   curry paste
2 leeks, trimmed and sliced
¾ cup canned diced tomatoes

1 small head cauliflower, broken
   into florets
8 ounces small new potatoes
2½ cups hot chicken stock
5 cups spinach
1 cup frozen peas
naan or rice (optional) to serve

1. Heat the oil in a large Dutch oven and brown the chicken all over. After 5 minutes, add the onion to the pot and cook for 5–10 minutes, until golden.

2. Add the curry paste and cook for 1 minute, then add the leeks, tomatoes, cauliflower, potatoes, and hot stock. Bring to a boil. Then reduce the heat, cover the Dutch oven, and simmer for 20–30 minutes until the chicken is cooked and the potatoes are tender.

3. Add the spinach and peas and cook for 5 minutes or until heated through. Serve with naan or rice, if desired.

Chicken Cacciatore

Preparation Time 5 minutes • Cooking Time 40 minutes • Serves 4 • Per Serving 327 calories, 17g fat (4g saturated), 3g carbohydrates, 1,300mg sodium • Gluten Free • Dairy Free • Easy

2 tablespoons olive oil
8 boneless, skinless chicken thighs
2 garlic cloves, crushed
1 teaspoon dried thyme
1 teaspoon dried tarragon
⅔ cup white wine*
1 (14½-ounce) can diced tomatoes
12 ripe black olives, pitted
12 capers, rinsed and drained
ground black pepper
brown rice and fava beans or peas
   to serve

1. Heat the oil in a flameproof Dutch oven over high heat. Add the chicken and brown all over. Reduce the heat and add the garlic, thyme, tarragon, and wine to the pot. Stir for 1 minute, then add the tomatoes and season with black pepper.

2. Bring to a boil, then reduce the heat, cover the pot, and simmer for 20 minutes or until the chicken is tender.

3. Lift the chicken out of the pot and put to one side. Simmer the sauce for 5 minutes or until thickened, add the olives and capers, stir well, and cook for another 2–3 minutes.

4. Return the chicken to the sauce. Serve with brown rice and fava beans or peas.

* This recipe is not suitable for children because it contains alcohol.

HEARTY
MEATS

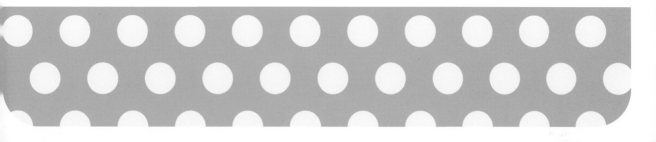

Beef Casserole with Black Olives

Preparation Time 20 minutes • Cooking Time 2 hours 10 minutes • Serves 6 • Per Serving 704 calories, 45g fat (13g saturated), 9g carbohydrates, 3,300mg sodium • Dairy Free • Easy

⅓ cup olive oil

2½ pounds boneless beef chuck uor beef round, cut into 1½-inch cubes

12 ounces unsmoked lean bacon, rind removed and sliced into thin strips

4 onions, coarsely chopped

3 large garlic cloves

2 tablespoons tomato paste

½ cup brandy*

1 tablespoon all-purpose flour

⅔ cup red wine*

1¼ cups beef stock

1 bouquet garni (see page 19)

8 ounces flat mushrooms, quartered if large

¾ cup ripe black olives, pitted

fresh Italian parsley sprigs to garnish (optional)

1. Heat 3 tablespoons oil in a large Dutch oven over high heat. Cook the beef in batches until browned all over; remove and keep warm. Add the bacon and sauté until golden brown. Put to one side with the beef.

2. Add the remaining oil and cook the onions over medium heat for 10–15 minutes, until golden brown. Add the garlic, sauté for 30 seconds. Then add the tomato paste and cook, stirring, for 1–2 minutes. Add the brandy and stir.

3. Preheat the oven to 350°F. Bring the casserole to a boil and simmer to reduce by half. Add the flour and mix until smooth. Pour in the wine, bring back to a boil, and simmer for 1 minute. Put the beef and bacon back into the casserole, and then add enough stock to barely cover the meat. Add the bouquet garni. Bring to a boil, cover, put into the oven, and cook for 1¼–1½ hours, until the beef is tender. Add the mushrooms and cook for another 4–5 minutes.

4. Just before serving, remove the bouquet garni and stir in the black olives. Serve hot, garnished with parsley, if desired.

* This recipe is not suitable for children because it contains alcohol.

FREEZING TIP

To freeze *Complete the recipe to the end of step 3. Cool quickly and put into a freezerproof container. Seal and freeze for up to one month.*
To use *Thaw overnight at cool room temperature. Preheat the oven to 350°F. Bring slowly to a boil on the stove. Cover and reheat in the oven for 20–25 minutes. Complete the recipe.*

Braised Beef with Bacon and Mushrooms

Preparation Time 20 minutes • Cooking Time about 3½ hours • Serves 4 • Per Serving 541 calories, 25g fat (9g saturated), 30g carbohydrates, 1,600mg sodium • Dairy Free • Easy

6 ounces smoked lean bacon or smoked pancetta, cubed

2 leeks, trimmed and thickly sliced

1 tablespoon olive oil

1 pound chuck shoulder steak, cut into 2-inch pieces

1 large onion, finely chopped

2 carrots, thickly sliced

2 parsnips, thickly sliced

1 tablespoon all-purpose flour

1¼ cups red wine*

1¼ cups water

1–2 tablespoons red currant jelly

4 ounces cremini mushrooms, halved

ground black pepper

freshly chopped Italian parsley to garnish

1. Preheat the oven to 340°F. Sauté the pancetta or bacon in a shallow Dutch oven for 2–3 minutes, until golden brown. Add the leeks and cook for another 2 minutes or until they are just beginning to brown. Remove with a slotted spoon and set aside.

2. Heat the oil in the casserole. Sauté the beef in batches for 2–3 minutes, until golden brown on all sides. Remove and set aside. Add the onion and sauté over a gentle heat for 5 minutes or until golden brown. Stir in the carrots and parsnips and sauté for 1–2 minutes.

3. Put the beef back into the casserole and stir in the flour to soak up the juices. Gradually add the wine and the water, and then stir in the red currant jelly. Season with black pepper and bring to a boil. Cover with a tight-fitting lid and cook in the oven for 2 hours.

4. Stir in the leeks, pancetta, and mushrooms, cover, and cook for 1 hour more, or until everything is tender. Serve hot, sprinkled with chopped parsley.

* This recipe is not suitable for children because it contains alcohol.

FREEZING TIP

To freeze *Complete the recipe to the end of step 4, without the garnish. Put into a freezerproof container, cool and freeze for up to three months.*

To use *Thaw overnight at cool room temperature. Preheat the oven to 350°F. Bring to a boil on the stove. Cover tightly and reheat in the oven for about 30 minutes or until piping hot.*

Beef Jambalaya

Preparation Time 10 minutes • Cooking Time 40 minutes • Serves 4 • Per Serving 554 calories, 30g fat (9g saturated), 40g carbohydrates, 1,800mg sodium • Gluten Free • Dairy Free • Easy

12 ounces tenderloin steak, cut into thin strips

4 teaspoons mild chili powder

1 teaspoon ground black pepper

about ⅓ cup olive oil

4 ounces chorizo sausage, sliced and cut into strips, or diced

2 celery sticks, cut into 2-inch strips

2 red bell peppers, seeded and cut into 2-inch strips

1 medium onion, coarsely chopped

2 garlic cloves, crushed

1⅓ cups long-grain white rice

1 tablespoon tomato paste

1 tablespoon ground ginger

2 teaspoons Cajun spice mix

3½ cups beef stock

8 large cooked shrimp, peeled and deveined (see page 71)

salt and ground black pepper

mixed salad to serve

1. Put the steak into a plastic sandwich bag with 1 teaspoon chili powder and the black pepper, seal, and shake to mix.

2. Heat 1 tablespoon oil in a large, heavy skillet and cook the chorizo until golden brown. Add the celery and red bell peppers to the pan and cook for 3–4 minutes, until just beginning to soften and brown. Remove from the pan and put to one side. Add 2 tablespoons oil to the pan and cook the steak in batches; put to one side and keep warm.

3. Add a little more oil to the skillet, if needed, and cook the onion until transparent. Add the garlic, rice, tomato paste, remaining chili powder, ground ginger, and Cajun spice mix, then cook for 2 minutes or until the rice turns translucent. Stir in the stock, season with salt, and bring to a boil. Reduce the heat, cover the pan, and simmer for about 20 minutes, stirring occasionally, or until the rice is tender and most of the liquid has been absorbed (add a little more water during cooking if needed).

4. Add the reserved steak, chorizo, red bell peppers, and celery, and the shrimp. Heat gently, stirring, until piping hot. Adjust the seasoning and serve with a salad.

COOK'S TIP

Jambalaya is a rice-based dish from Louisiana that traditionally contains spicy sausage, chicken, ham, or shrimp and plenty of chili.

Chunky One-Pot Bolognese

Preparation Time 15 minutes • Cooking Time about 1 hour • Serves 6 • Per Serving 506 calories, 31g fat (11g saturated), 40g carbohydrates, 1,500mg sodium • Dairy Free • Easy

3 tablespoons olive oil

2 large red onions, finely diced

a few fresh rosemary sprigs

1 large eggplant, finely diced

8 plump Italian-style link sausages

1½ cups full-bodied red wine*

3 cups canned tomato puree or tomato sauce

¼ cup tomato paste

1¼ cups hot vegetable stock

8 ounces small dried pasta, such as orecchiette

salt and ground black pepper

1. Heat 2 tablespoons oil in a large shallow nonstick saucepan. Add the onions and rosemary and cook over gentle heat for 10 minutes or until soft and golden brown.

2. Add the eggplant and remaining oil and cook over medium heat for 8–10 minutes, until soft and golden brown.

3. Meanwhile, pull the skin off the sausages and divide each into four chunks. Put the eggplant mixture on a plate and add the sausage chunks to the hot pan. You won't need any extra oil.

4. Stir the sausage pieces over high heat for 6–8 minutes, until golden brown and beginning to turn crisp at the edges. Pour in the wine and let simmer for 6–8 minutes, until only a little liquid remains. Put the eggplant mixture back into the pan, along with the tomato puree or sauce, tomato paste, and hot stock.

5. Stir the pasta into the liquid, cover, and then simmer for 20 minutes or until the pasta is cooked. Taste and season with salt and black pepper, if necessary.

* This recipe is not suitable for children because it contains alcohol.

FREEZING TIP

*To **freeze** Freeze leftover portions separately. Complete the recipe to the end of step 4. Add the pasta and cook for 10 minutes—it will continue to cook right through when you reheat the meat sauce. Cool, put into a freezerproof container and freeze for up to three months.*

*To **use** Thaw overnight at cool room temperature, put into a saucepan and add ⅔ cup water. Bring to a boil, then simmer gently for 10 minutes or until the sauce is hot and the pasta is cooked.*

One-Pot Spicy Beef

Preparation Time 10 minutes • Cooking Time about 40 minutes • Serves 4 • Per Serving 380 calories, 13g fat (8g saturated), 36g carbohydrates, 1,800mg sodium • Gluten Free • Dairy Free • Easy

2 teaspoons sunflower oil
1 large onion, coarsely chopped
2 tablespoons water
1 garlic clove, finely chopped
1 small red chili, finely chopped (see page 15)
2 red bell peppers, seeded and coarsely chopped
2 celery sticks, diced
1 pound ground round or ground sirloin beef
1 (14½-ounce) can diced tomatoes
3 cups canned mixed beans (such as red kidney beans, pinto beans, and chickpeas), drained and rinsed
1–2 teaspoons Tabasco sauce
salsa to serve (see Cook's Tip)

1. Heat the oil in a large skillet. Add the onion to the skillet with the water and cook for 10 minutes or until softened. Add the garlic and chili and cook for 1–2 minutes, until golden brown. Add the red bell peppers and celery and cook for 5 minutes.

2. Add the beef to the skillet and brown all over. Add the tomatoes, beans, and Tabasco. Simmer for 20 minutes. Serve with the salsa.

COOK'S TIP
Salsa
Put ½ ripe avocado, peeled, pitted, and coarsely chopped, 4 coarsely chopped tomatoes, 1 teaspoon olive oil, and the juice of ½ lime into a bowl and stir well. Serve at once.

Peppered Winter Stew

Preparation Time 20 minutes • Cooking Time 2¾ hours • Serves 6 • Per Serving 540 calories, 24g fat (7g saturated), 24g carbohydrates, 1,500mg sodium • Dairy Free • Easy

¼ cup all-purpose flour

2 pounds boneless beef chuck, venison, or lamb, cut into 1½-inch cubes

⅓ cup olive oil

8 ounces pearl onions or shallots, peeled with root end intact

2 onions, finely chopped

4 garlic cloves, crushed

2 tablespoons tomato paste

½ cup red wine vinegar

3 cups (1 bottle) red wine*

2 tablespoons red currant jelly

1 small bunch of fresh thyme, plus extra sprigs to garnish (optional)

4 bay leaves

1 tablespoon coarsely ground black pepper

6 whole cloves

2 pounds mixed root vegetables (such as carrots, parsnips, turnips, and celeriac), cut into 1½-inch chunks; carrots cut a little smaller

2½–3½ cups beef stock

salt

1. Preheat the oven to 350°F. Put the flour into a plastic sandwich bag and season with salt and black pepper. Add the meat and toss to coat.

2. Heat 3 tablespoons oil in a large Dutch oven over medium heat and brown the meat well in small batches. Remove and set aside.

3. Heat the remaining oil and sauté the pearl onions or shallots for 5 minutes or until golden brown. Add the chopped onion and the garlic and cook, stirring, until soft and golden brown. Add the tomato paste and cook for another 2 minutes. Add the vinegar and wine and bring to a boil. Simmer for 10 minutes.

4. Add the red currant jelly, thyme, bay leaves, 1 tablespoon coarsely ground black pepper, the cloves, and meat to the pot with the vegetables and enough stock to barely cover the meat and vegetables. Bring to a boil, then reduce the heat, cover the pot, and cook in the oven for 1¾–2¼ hours, until the meat is tender. Serve hot and garnish with thyme sprigs, if desired.

* This recipe is not suitable for children because it contains alcohol.

FREEZING TIP

To freeze *Complete the recipe to the end of step 4, without the garnish. Cool quickly and put in a freezerproof container. Seal and freeze for up to one month.*

To use *Thaw overnight at cool room temperature. Preheat the oven to 350°F. Put into a Dutch oven and add an extra ⅔ cup beef stock. Bring to a boil. Cover and reheat for 30 minutes.*

Hearty Ham Stew

Preparation Time 15 minutes • Cooking Time 1 hour 10 minutes • Serves 4 • Per Serving 680 calories, 30g fat (11g saturated), 41g carbohydrates, 6,300mg sodium • Gluten Free • Easy

1 tablespoon olive oil

2½ pounds smoked ham

8 shallots, blanched in boiling water, drained, peeled, and chopped into chunks

3 carrots, chopped into chunks

3 celery sticks, chopped into chunks

4 large red-skinned or white round potatoes, unpeeled

2 cups apple juice

2 cups hot vegetable stock

½ small Savoy cabbage, shredded

2 tablespoons butter

1. Preheat the oven to 375°F. Heat the oil in a large Dutch oven. Add the ham and cook for 5 minutes or until brown all over. Remove from the pan.

2. Add the shallots, carrots, and celery to the pot and sauté for 3–4 minutes, until starting to soften.

3. Return the ham to the pot. Chop the potatoes into quarters and add to the pot with the apple juice and hot stock. Cover and bring to a boil. Transfer to the oven and cook for 50 minutes or until the meat is cooked through and the vegetables are tender.

4. Remove from the oven and put the pot back on the stove over low heat. Add the cabbage and stir into the pot. Simmer for 2–3 minutes, then stir in the butter and serve.

Spicy Pork and Bean Stew

Preparation Time 15 minutes • Cooking Time 50–55 minutes • Serves 4 • Per Serving 373 calories, 14g fat (3g saturated), 32g carbohydrates, 1,200mg sodium • Dairy Free • Easy

3 tablespoons olive oil
1 pound pork cutlets, cubed
1 red onion, sliced
2 leeks, trimmed and cut into chunks
2 celery sticks, cut into chunks
1 tablespoon harissa paste
1 tablespoon tomato paste
1 (14½-ounce) can cherry tomatoes or diced tomatoes
1¼ cups hot vegetable or chicken stock
1 (14½-ounce) can cannellini beans, drained and rinsed
1 marinated red bell pepper, sliced
salt and ground black pepper
freshly chopped Italian parsley to garnish
Greek yogurt and lemon wedges to serve

1. Preheat the oven to 350°F. Heat 2 tablespoons oil in a Dutch oven and sauté the pork in batches until golden brown. Remove from the pot and set aside.

2. Heat the remaining oil in the pot and sauté the onion for 5–10 minutes, until softened. Add the leeks and celery and cook for about 5 minutes. Return the pork to the pot and add the harissa and tomato paste. Cook for 1–2 minutes, stirring all the time. Add the tomatoes and hot stock. Season well with salt and black pepper. Bring to a boil. Transfer to the oven and cook for 25 minutes.

3. Add the drained beans and marinated pepper to the mixture and put back into the oven for 5 minutes to warm through. Garnish with parsley and serve with a dollop of Greek yogurt and lemon wedges for squeezing over the stew.

COOK'S TIP
For a simple accompaniment, serve with chunks of crusty French bread or whole-wheat bread.

Honey Pork with Roast Potatoes and Apples

Preparation Time 20 minutes • Cooking Time 1 hour 40 minutes, plus resting • Serves 4 • Per Serving 830 calories, 55g fat (19g saturated), 40g carbohydrates, 400mg sodium • Gluten Free • Easy

2¼ pounds loin of pork, with skin and four bones

1 teaspoon salt

¼ cup olive oil

2 tablespoons butter

1½ pounds new potatoes, scrubbed and halved

1 large onion, cut into eight wedges

1 tablespoon honey mixed with 1 tablespoon whole-grain mustard

2 Pippin apples, cored and each cut into six wedges

12 fresh sage leaves

¾ cup dry hard cider* or apple juice

ground black pepper

1. Preheat the oven to 475°F. Put the pork on a board and use a paring knife to score the skin into thin strips, cutting about halfway into the fat underneath. Rub the salt and 2 tablespoons oil over the skin and season well with black pepper. Put the meat on a rack, skin side up, over a large roasting pan (or just put the pork into the pan).

2. Roast for 25 minutes. Turn the oven down to 375°F and continue to roast for 15 minutes. Add the remaining oil and the butter to the roasting pan. Put the potatoes and onion around the meat, season, and continue to roast for 45 minutes.

3. Brush the meat with the honey and mustard mixture. Add the apples and sage leaves to the pan and roast for another 15 minutes or until the pork is cooked.

4. Remove the pork from the pan and wrap completely with aluminum foil, then let rest for 10 minutes. Put the potatoes, onions, and apples into a warmed serving dish and put back in the oven to keep warm.

5. Put the roasting pan on the stove, add the cider or apple juice, and stir well to make a thin gravy. Season.

6. Cut the meat away from the bone. Cut between each bone. Pull the crackling away from the meat and cut into strips. Carve the meat, giving each person some crackling and a bone to chew. Serve with the gravy and potatoes, onion, and apples.

* This recipe is not suitable for children if it contains alcohol.

Savory Pudding

Preparation Time 15 minutes, plus soaking • Cooking Time 1–1¼ hours • Serves 6 • Per Serving 397 calories, 27g fat (15g saturated), 17g carbohydrates, 2,200mg sodium • Easy

5–6 thick slices white bread (such as sourdough), crusts left on
6 tablespoons butter, softened
2 tablespoons Dijon mustard
8 ounces sliced ham, coarsely chopped
1⅓ cups shredded sharp cheddar
2½ cups whole milk
5 extra-large eggs, beaten
a pinch of freshly grated nutmeg
2 tablespoons freshly chopped herbs, such as parsley, marjoram, or thyme
salt and ground black pepper
green salad to serve

1. Spread the bread generously with butter and sparingly with mustard. Put half the slices into the bottom of a 2-quart ovenproof dish. Top with the ham and half the cheese, then with the remaining bread, butter side up.

2. Whisk together the milk, eggs, nutmeg, and plenty of salt and black pepper. Stir in the herbs, then slowly pour the mixture over the bread. Sprinkle the remaining cheese on top and let soak for 15 minutes. Meanwhile, preheat the oven to 350°F.

3. Put the dish into a roasting pan and fill halfway up the sides with lukewarm water. Then cook for 1–1¼ hours, until puffed up, golden brown and just set to the center. Serve immediately, with a salad.

TRY SOMETHING DIFFERENT

For a vegetarian alternative, omit the ham and use 2¼ cups cheese, such as Gruyère (see Cook's Tip on page 130). Add three-quarters of the cheese over the first layer of bread and sprinkle the remaining cheese on top.

Pork, Garlic, and Basil Risotto

Preparation Time 15 minutes • Cooking Time 50 minutes • Serves 6 • Per Serving 431 calories,
18g fat (6g saturated), 28g carbohydrates, 700mg sodium • Easy

6 thin pork cutlets
6 prosciutto slices
6 fresh basil leaves
¼ cup all-purpose flour
6 tablespoons unsalted butter
1 medium onion, finely chopped
2 garlic cloves, crushed
1 cup risotto rice
2 cups white wine*
2 cups hot chicken stock
3 tablespoons ready-made pesto
(see page 23)
½ cup grated Parmesan
¼ cup freshly chopped Italian
parsley
salt and ground black pepper

1. Preheat the oven to 350°F. If needed, pound the cutlets carefully with a rolling pin until they are wafer thin. Lay a slice of prosciutto on each cutlet and put a basil leaf on top. Hold in place with a wooden toothpick. Season and dip in the flour, dusting off any excess.

2. Melt a small piece of the butter in a deep ovenproof saucepan and quickly pan-fry the cutlets in batches for 2–3 minutes on each side, until lightly golden brown. Melt a little more butter for each batch. You will need about half the butter at this stage. Remove the cutlets and keep warm, covered, in the oven.

3. Melt another 2 tablespoons butter in the pan and sauté the onion for about 10 minutes or until soft and golden brown. Add the garlic and rice and stir well. Add the wine and hot stock. Bring to a boil, and then put in the oven and bake, uncovered, for 20 minutes.

4. Stir in the pesto, Parmesan, and parsley. Push the browned cutlets into the rice, cover, and put the pan back in the oven for another 5 minutes or until the rice has completely absorbed the liquid and the cutlets are cooked through and piping hot.

* This recipe is not suitable for children because it contains alcohol.

TRY SOMETHING DIFFERENT
Use turkey or veal cutlets instead of pork.

Pork and Apple Hotpot

Preparation Time 15 minutes • Cooking Time 2–2¼ hours • Serves 4 • Per Serving 592 calories, 18g fat (7g saturated), 56g carbohydrates, 1,000mg sodium • Easy

1 tablespoon olive oil

2 pounds pork shoulder cutlets

3 onions, cut into wedges

1 large Granny Smith apple, peeled, cored, and thickly sliced

1 tablespoon all-purpose flour

2½ cups hot, weak chicken or vegetable stock

¼ Savoy cabbage, sliced

2 fresh thyme sprigs

8 red-skinned or white round potatoes (about 2 pounds), cut into ¾-inch slices

2 tablespoons butter

salt and ground black pepper

1. Preheat the oven to 350°F. Heat the oil in a large, nonstick flameproof Dutch oven until hot, and then cook the pork cutlets, two at a time, for 5 minutes or until golden brown all over. Remove the pork from the pot and set aside.

2. In the same pot, sauté the onions for 10 minutes or until soft—add a little water if they start to stick. Stir in the apple and cook for 1 minute, then add the flour to soak up the juices. Gradually add the hot stock and stir until smooth. Season with salt and black pepper. Stir in the cabbage and add the pork.

3. Throw in the thyme, overlap the potato slices on top, and then dot with the butter. Cover with a tight-fitting lid and cook near the top of the oven for 1 hour. Remove the lid and cook for another 30–45 minutes, until the potatoes are tender and golden brown.

COOK'S TIP

Put the stew under the broiler for 2–3 minutes so the potatoes become more crispy, if desired.

FREEZING TIP

__To freeze__ Cool quickly, and then freeze for up to three months.
__To use__ Thaw overnight at cool room temperature. Preheat the oven to 350°F. Pour ¼ cup hot stock over the stew. Cover and reheat for 30 minutes or until piping hot. Uncover and crisp the potatoes under the broiler for 2–3 minutes.

Ribs and Beans in a Sticky Barbecue Sauce

Preparation time 10 minutes • Cooking time 1¼ hours • Serves 4 • Per serving 620 calories, 25g fat (10g saturated), 53g carbohydrates, 1,000mg sodium • Easy

8 meaty pork spareribs
1 large onion, chopped
2 large garlic cloves, chopped
¼ cup packed light brown sugar
1 tablespoon French mustard
¼ cup sun-dried tomato paste
⅔ cup tomato puree or tomato sauce
¼ cup malt vinegar
¼ cup ketchup
2 tablespoons Worcestershire sauce
2⅓ cups dry hard cider* or apple juice
2 (15-ounce) cans black-eyed peas, drained and rinsed
¼ cup freshly chopped parsley
salt and ground black pepper

1. Preheat the over to 400°F. Trim the spareribs of excess fat, if necessary, and season with salt and black pepper.

2. Put the onion, garlic, sugar, mustard, tomato paste, tomato puree or sauce, vinegar, ketchup, and Worcestershire sauce into a large roasting pan and stir well. Add the spareribs and stir to coat in the sauce.

3. Bake in the oven for 30 minutes, and then turn the ribs over and cook for another 30 minutes, until they are crisp and brown.

4. Add the cider and stir to mix well with the sauce, scraping up the sediment from the bottom of the pan. Add the black-eyed peas, stir, and return to the oven for another 15 minutes. Sprinkle with the chopped parsley to serve.

* This recipe is not suitable for children if it contains alcohol.

TRY SOMETHING DIFFERENT
Use canned navy beans or pinto beans instead of black-eyed peas.

Belly of Pork with Cider and Rosemary

Preparation Time 30 minutes, plus cooling and chilling • Cooking Time about 4½ hours • Serves 8 •
Per Serving 694 calories, 52g fat (19g saturated), 9g carbohydrates, 500mg sodium • Easy

4½-pound piece pork belly roast,
   on the bone
2¼ cups medium cider* or apple
   juice
2½ cups hot chicken stock
6–8 fresh rosemary sprigs
3 fat garlic cloves, halved
2 tablespoons olive oil
grated zest and juice of 1 large
   orange and 1 lemon
1 teaspoon salt
3 tablespoons packed light brown
   sugar
2 tablespoons butter, softened,
   mixed with 1 tablespoon all-
   purpose flour
ground black pepper
mixed vegetables to serve

1. Preheat the oven to 300°F. Put the pork, skin side up, in a roasting pan just large enough to hold it. Add the cider or apple juice, hot stock, and half the rosemary. Bring to a boil on the stove. Cover with aluminum foil and bake in the oven for 4 hours. Let cool in the cooking liquid.

2. Strip the leaves from the remaining rosemary and chop. Put into a mortar with the garlic, oil, orange and lemon zest, salt, and 1 tablespoon sugar. Pound with a pestle for 3–4 minutes to make a coarse paste.

3. Remove the pork from the pan (keep the cooking liquid) and slice off the rind from the top layer of fat. Put to one side. Score the fat into a diamond pattern and rub in the rosemary paste. Cover loosely with plastic wrap and chill until required.

4. Pat the rind dry with paper towels and put it (fat side up) on an aluminum foil-lined baking sheet. Cook under a hot broiler, about 4 inches away from the heat, for 5 minutes. Turn over, sprinkle lightly with salt, then broil for 7–10 minutes until crisp. Cool, then cut the crackling into rough pieces.

5. Make the gravy. Strain the cooking liquid into a saucepan. Add the orange and lemon juice and the remaining sugar, bring to a boil, and simmer until reduced by half. Whisk the butter mixture into the liquid and boil for 4–5 minutes, until thickened. Put to one side.

6. When almost ready to serve, preheat the oven to 425°F. Cook the pork, uncovered, in a roasting pan for 20 minutes or until piping hot. Wrap the crackling in aluminum foil and warm in the oven for the last 5 minutes of the cooking time. Heat the gravy on the stove. Carve the pork into slices and serve with the crackling, gravy, and vegetables.

This recipe is not suitable for children if it contains alcohol.

Warming Winter Casserole

Preparation Time 20 minutes • Cooking Time 1 hour • Serves 4 • Per Serving 407 calories,
16g fat (3g saturated), 32g carbohydrates, 1,000mg sodium • Gluten Free • Dairy Free • Easy

2 tablespoons olive oil

1 pound pork tenderloin, cubed

1 onion, finely chopped

2 garlic cloves, finely chopped

1 teaspoon ground cinnamon

1 tablespoon ground coriander

**1-inch piece fresh ginger, peeled
and grated**

**2 cups canned mixed beans (such
as kidney beans, pinto beans,
and chickpeas), drained and
rinsed**

**1 red bell pepper, seeded and
sliced**

**¼ cup dried apricots, coarsely
chopped**

1¼ cups chicken stock

¼ cup slivered almonds, toasted

salt and ground black pepper

**freshly chopped Italian parsley
to garnish**

brown rice to serve

1. Heat 1 tablespoon oil in a Dutch oven, add the pork in batches, and sauté until brown all over. Remove and set aside. Add the remaining oil, then add the onion and cook for 10 minutes or until softened. Return the pork to the pot, add the garlic, spices, and ginger, and cook for 2 minutes.

2. Add the mixed beans, red bell pepper, apricots, and stock. Season well with salt and black pepper, and then stir and bring to a boil. Reduce the heat to the lowest setting and simmer, covered, for 40 minutes, adding a little extra stock if it begins to look dry.

3. Check the seasoning and sprinkle with the almonds, then garnish with the parsley and serve with brown rice.

**TRY SOMETHING
DIFFERENT**

*Instead of pork, use the same
quantity of lean lamb, such as leg,
trimmed of excess fat and cut into
1-inch cubes.*

Potato and Chorizo Tortilla

Preparation Time 15 minutes • Cooking Time about 25 minutes • Serves 4 • Per Serving 566 calories,
42g fat (8g saturated), 23g carbohydrates, 1,200mg sodium • Gluten Free • Dairy Free • Easy

⅓ cup olive oil

4 red-skinned or white round
   potatoes, thinly sliced

2 onions, thinly sliced

2 garlic cloves, chopped

2 ounces chorizo sausage, cut
   into strips

6 extra-large eggs

4 soft tortilla shells

salt and ground black pepper

1. Heat the oil in a 7-inch nonstick skillet. Add the potatoes, onion, and garlic, and stir to coat. Cover the skillet, then cook gently for 15 minutes, stirring occasionally, or until the potato is soft. Season with salt.

2. Add the chorizo to the skillet. Beat the eggs and season with salt and black pepper, then pour into the pan and cook for about 5 minutes or until the edges are beginning to brown and the egg looks about three-quarters set.

3. Put the tortilla under a hot broiler and quickly brown the top. Remove from the heat and let cool. Loosen the edges, cut into wedges, and serve on the side.

Pan-Fried Chorizo and Potato

Preparation Time 10 minutes • Cooking Time 30 minutes • Serves 4 • Per Serving 553 calories, 36g fat (12g saturated), 32g carbohydrates, 3,400mg sodium • Gluten Free • Dairy Free • Easy

2 tablespoons olive oil

4 red-skinned or white round potatoes, cut into 1-inch cubes

2 red onions, sliced

1 red bell pepper, seeded and chopped

1 teaspoon paprika

12-ounce piece of chorizo sausage, skinned and cut into chunky slices

2 cups cherry tomatoes

½ cup dry sherry*

2 tablespoons freshly chopped Italian parsley

1. Heat the oil in a large, heavy skillet over medium heat. Add the potatoes and sauté for 7–10 minutes, until lightly browned, turning regularly.

2. Reduce the heat, add the onions and red bell pepper, and continue to cook for 10 minutes, stirring from time to time, or until they have softened but not browned.

3. Add the paprika and chorizo and cook for 5 minutes, stirring from time to time.

4. Add the cherry tomatoes and pour in the sherry. Stir everything together and cook for 5 minutes, or until the sherry has reduced and the tomatoes have softened and warmed through.

5. Sprinkle the chopped parsley over the top and serve.

* This recipe is not suitable for children because it contains alcohol.

Turkish Lamb Stew

Preparation Time 10 minutes • Cooking Time 1½–2 hours • Serves 4 • Per Serving 389 calories, 20g fat (7g saturated), 28g carbohydrates, 1,200mg sodium • Gluten Free • Dairy Free • Easy

2 tablespoons olive oil

1 pound lean lamb cutlets, cubed

1 red onion, sliced

1 garlic clove, crushed

1 potato, quartered

1 (14½-ounce) can diced plum tomatoes

1 red bell pepper, seeded and sliced

1 cup canned chickpeas, drained and rinsed

1 eggplant, cut into chunks

¾ cup lamb stock

1 tablespoon red wine vinegar

1 teaspoon each freshly chopped thyme, rosemary, and oregano

8 ripe black olives, pitted and halved

salt and ground black pepper

1. Heat 1 tablespoon oil in a Dutch oven and brown the lamb over high heat. Reduce the heat and add the remaining oil, onion, and garlic, and then cook until soft.

2. Preheat the oven to 350°F. Add the potato, tomatoes, red bell pepper, chickpeas, eggplant, stock, vinegar, and herbs to the pot. Season, stir, and bring to a boil. Cover the pot, transfer to the oven and bake for 1–1½ hours until the lamb is tender.

3. About 15 minutes before the end of the cooking time, add the olives.

Lamb, Prune, and Almond Tagine

Preparation Time 20 minutes, plus marinating • Cooking Time 2½ hours • Serves 6 • Per Serving 652 calories, 44g fat (16g saturated), 31g carbohydrates, 600mg sodium • Gluten Free • Easy

2 teaspoons coriander seeds

2 teaspoons cumin seeds

2 teaspoons chili powder

1 tablespoon paprika

1 tablespoon ground turmeric

5 garlic cloves, chopped

⅓ cup olive oil

3 pounds lamb cutlets

⅓ cup ghee or clarified butter (see Cook's Tip)

2 large onions, finely chopped

1 carrot, coarsely chopped

3½ cups lamb stock

2⅓ cups prunes

4 cinnamon sticks

4 bay leaves

½ cup ground almonds (almond meal)

12 shallots

1 tablespoon honey

salt and ground black pepper

toasted blanched almonds and freshly chopped Italian parsley to garnish

couscous to serve

1. Using a mortar and pestle or a blender, combine the coriander and cumin seeds, chili powder, paprika, turmeric, garlic, and ¼ cup oil. Coat the lamb with the paste, then cover and chill for at least 5 hours.

2. Preheat the oven to 350°F. Melt 2 tablespoons ghee or clarified butter in a large Dutch oven. Add the onions and carrot and cook until soft. Remove and put to one side. Cook the paste-coated lamb on both sides in the remaining ghee or butter. Add a little of the stock and bring to a boil, scraping up the sediment from the bottom of the pot. Put the onions and carrot back in the pot and add one-third of the prunes. Add the remaining stock with the cinnamon sticks, bay leaves, and ground almonds. Season, cover, and bake in the oven for 2 hours or until the meat is really tender.

3. Meanwhile, sauté the shallots in the remaining oil and the honey until they turn a deep golden brown. Add to the pot 30–40 minutes before the end of the cooking time.

4. Take the lamb out of the sauce and put to one side. Bring the sauce to a boil, then reduce to a thick consistency. Put the lamb back in the casserole, add the remaining prunes, and simmer for 3–4 minutes. Garnish with the almonds and parsley. Serve hot with couscous.

COOK'S TIP

To make clarified butter, heat butter in a pan without letting it brown. Skim off the foam; the solids will sink. Pour the clear butter into a bowl through a lined strainer. Let stand for 10 minutes. Pour into a bowl, leaving any sediment behind. Cool. Store in a jar in the refrigerator for up to six months.

Italian Braised Leg of Lamb

Preparation Time 15 minutes • Cooking Time about 5 hours • Serves 6 • Per Serving 400 calories, 18g fat (6g saturated), 17g carbohydrates, 700mg sodium • Gluten Free • Dairy Free • Easy

5-pound boneless leg of lamb joint
¼ cup olive oil
6 onions (about 1½ pounds),
  coarsely chopped
1 each red, orange, and yellow bell
  pepper, seeded and coarsely
  chopped
2 red chilis, seeded and finely
  chopped (see page 15)
1 garlic bulb, cloves separated and
  peeled
3 tablespoons dried oregano
3 cups (1 bottle) dry white wine*
3 (14½-ounce) cans cherry
  tomatoes or diced tomatoes
salt and ground black pepper

1. Preheat the oven to 350°F. Season the lamb with salt and black pepper. Heat 2 tablespoons oil in a large, deep Dutch oven and brown the meat well. Remove and set aside. Wipe the pot clean.

2. Heat the remaining oil in the pot and sauté the onions, bell peppers, chilis, garlic, and oregano over medium heat for 10–15 minutes, until the onions are translucent and golden brown. Stir in the wine and tomatoes and bring to a boil. Simmer for 10 minutes.

3. Put the lamb on top of the vegetables and season. Baste the meat with the sauce and cover the casserole tightly with aluminum foil and a lid. Cook in the oven for 4 hours, basting occasionally.

4. Uncover and cook for another 30 minutes. Serve the lamb carved into thick slices with the sauce spooned over the meat.

* This recipe is not suitable for children because it contains alcohol.

VEG
OUT

Spinach and Cheese Lasagna

Preparation Time 30 minutes • Cooking Time 50–55 minutes • Serves 6 • Per Serving 442 calories, 27g fat (14g saturated), 32g carbohydrates, 1,600mg sodium • Vegetarian • Easy

4 cups fresh or 1 cup frozen spinach, thawed

1 cup fresh basil, coarsely chopped

1 cup ricotta cheese (see Cook's Tip on page 130)

5 pieces marinated artichokes, drained and chopped

1½ cups ready-made cheesy white sauce (see page 64)

6 ounces Dolcelatte cheese, coarsely diced

9 fresh egg lasagna noodles

¼ cup pine nuts, toasted

tomato salad to serve

1. Preheat the oven to 350°F. Chop the spinach finely (if it was frozen, squeeze out the excess liquid). Put into a bowl with the basil, ricotta cheese, artichokes, and ⅓ cup cheese sauce. Mix well.

2. Beat the Dolcelatte into the remaining cheese sauce. Layer the ricotta mixture, lasagna noodles, and cheese sauce into a 9 x 9-inch ovenproof dish. Repeat to use up the remainder.

3. Bake the lasagna for 40 minutes. Sprinkle the pine nuts over the top and put back in the oven for another 10–15 minutes, until golden brown. Serve with a tomato salad.

COOK'S TIP

Italian Dolcelatte cheese has a much milder flavor than Stilton or Roquefort; it also has a deliciously rich, creamy texture.

Butternut Squash and Spinach Lasagna

Preparation Time 30 minutes • Cooking Time about 1 hour • Serves 6 • Per Serving 273 calories, 17g fat (7g saturated), 18g carbohydrates, 600mg sodium • Vegetarian • Easy

1 butternut squash, peeled, halved, seeded, and cut into 1¼-inch cubes

2 tablespoons olive oil

1 onion, sliced

2 tablespoons water

2 tablespoons butter

¼ cup all-purpose flour

2½ cups milk

1 cup ricotta cheese (see Cook's Tip on page 130)

1 teaspoon freshly grated nutmeg

1 (6-ounce) package baby spinach

6 fresh egg lasagna noodles

½ cup freshly grated pecorino cheese or Parmesan

salt and ground black pepper

1. Preheat the oven to 400°F. Put the squash into a roasting pan with the oil, onion, and 1 tablespoon water. Mix well and season to taste with salt and black pepper. Roast for 25 minutes, tossing halfway through.

2. To make the sauce, melt the butter in a saucepan. Stir in the flour and cook over medium heat for 1–2 minutes. Gradually add the milk, stirring constantly. Reduce the heat to a simmer and cook, stirring, for 5 minutes or until the sauce has thickened. Crumble the ricotta into the sauce and add the nutmeg. Mix together thoroughly and season with salt and black pepper.

3. Heat the remaining water in a saucepan. Add the spinach, cover, and cook until just wilted. Season generously.

4. Spoon the squash mixture into a 1½-quart ovenproof dish. Layer the spinach on top, cover with a third of the sauce, and then the lasagna noodles. Spoon the remaining sauce on top, season with salt and black pepper, and sprinkle with the grated cheese. Bake for about 30–35 minutes, until the cheese topping is golden brown and the pasta is cooked.

Artichoke and Mushroom Lasagna

Preparation Time 25 minutes • Cooking Time about 1½ hours • Serves 6 • Per serving 322 calories, 21g fat (11g saturated), 19g carbohydrates, 700mg sodium • Vegetarian • Easy

3 tablespoons olive oil

2 onions, coarsely chopped

3 garlic cloves, crushed

¼ cup walnuts

2½ pounds mixed mushrooms
   (such as brown-cap and button),
   coarsely chopped

8 cherry tomatoes

4 tablespoons butter, plus extra
   to grease

⅓ cup all-purpose flour

4½ cups whole milk

2 bay leaves

2 tablespoons lemon juice

8–10 fresh egg lasagna noodles

1 (14-ounce) can artichoke hearts
   in water, drained and halved

⅔ cup freshly grated Parmesan
   (see Cook's Tip on page 130)

salt and ground black pepper

fresh oregano sprigs to garnish
   (optional)

1. Heat the oil in a large saucepan and sauté the onions gently for 10 minutes, until soft. Add the garlic and walnuts and sauté for 3–4 minutes, until pale golden brown. Stir in the chopped mushrooms and cook for 10 minutes. Let the mixture simmer briskly for another 10 minutes or until all the liquid has evaporated. Add the tomatoes to the pan, and then remove from the heat and set aside.

2. Preheat the oven to 400°F. Melt the butter in a pan, add the flour, and stir over gentle heat for 1 minute. Slowly whisk in the milk until you have a smooth mixture. Bring to a boil, add the bay leaves, and then stir over gentle heat for 10 minutes, until thickened and smooth. Add the lemon juice and season to taste with salt and black pepper. Discard the bay leaves.

3. Grease a shallow, ovenproof dish and layer lasagna noodles over the bottom. Spoon half the mushroom mixture over the pasta, and then half the artichokes. Cover with a layer of lasagna noodles and half the sauce. Spoon the remaining mushroom mixture over the top, and then the remaining artichokes. Top with the remaining lasagna noodles. Stir the Parmesan into the remaining sauce and spoon evenly over the top of the lasagna.

4. Bake in the oven for 40–50 minutes, until golden brown and bubbling. Garnish with oregano sprigs, if using, and serve.

GET AHEAD

To prepare ahead Complete the recipe to the end of step 3. Then cool, cover, and chill for up to three hours.

To use Remove from the refrigerator about 30 minutes before cooking, and then complete the recipe.

Curried Coconut and Vegetable Rice

Preparation Time 15 minutes • Cooking Time 30 minutes, plus standing • Serves 6 • Per Serving 413 calories, 17g fat (2g saturated), 57g carbohydrates, 400mg sodium • Vegetarian • Gluten Free • Dairy Free • Easy

1 large eggplant, about 11 ounces

1 butternut squash, peeled and seeded

8 ounces green beans, trimmed

½ cup vegetable oil

1 large onion, chopped

1 tablespoon black mustard seeds

3 tablespoons korma paste

1¾ cups basmati or other long-grain rice

2 teaspoons salt

1¾ cups coconut milk

2½ cups water

1 (6-ounce) package baby spinach leaves

ground black pepper

1. Cut the eggplant and butternut squash into ¾-inch cubes. Slice the green beans into ¾-inch pieces.

2. Heat the oil in a large saucepan. Add the onion and cook for about 5 minutes or until a light golden brown. Add the mustard seeds and cook, stirring, until they begin to pop. Stir in the korma paste and cook for 1 minute.

3. Add the eggplant and cook, stirring, for 5 minutes. Add the butternut squash, beans, rice, and the salt, mixing well. Pour in the coconut milk and add the water. Bring to a boil, and then reduce the heat, cover the pan, and simmer for 15–18 minutes.

4. When the rice and vegetables are cooked, remove the lid, and put the spinach leaves on top. Cover, remove from the heat, and let stand for 5 minutes. Gently stir the wilted spinach through the rice, check the seasoning, and serve immediately.

Leek and Broccoli Casserole

Preparation Time 20 minutes • Cooking Time 45–55 minutes • Serves 6 • Per Serving 245 calories, 13g fat (4g saturated), 18g carbohydrates, 400mg sodium • Gluten Free • Easy

2 tablespoons olive oil

1 large red onion, cut into wedges

1 eggplant, chopped

2 leeks, trimmed and cut into chunks

1 broccoli head, cut into florets and stalks chopped

3 large flat mushrooms, chopped

5½ cups cherry tomatoes (about 1¾ pounds)

3 fresh rosemary sprigs, leaves chopped

1¼ cups boiling water

½ cup freshly grated Parmesan (see Cook's Tip on page 130)

salt and ground black pepper

1. Preheat the oven to 400°F. Heat the oil in a large flameproof dish, add the onion, eggplant, and leeks, and cook for 10–12 minutes, until golden and softened.

2. Add the broccoli, mushrooms, cherry tomatoes, half the rosemary, and the boiling water. Season with salt and black pepper. Stir well. Cover and bake in the oven for 30 minutes.

3. Meanwhile, put the Parmesan into a bowl. Add the remaining rosemary and season with black pepper. When the vegetables are cooked, remove the lid and sprinkle the Parmesan mixture on top. Bake, uncovered, in the oven for another 5–10 minutes, until the topping is golden brown.

TRY SOMETHING DIFFERENT
Use sliced zucchini instead of eggplant.

Lentil Casserole

Preparation Time 20 minutes • Cooking Time 1 hour • Serves 6 • Per Serving 239 calories,
6g fat (1g saturated), 36g carbohydrates, 400mg sodium • Vegetarian • Gluten Free • Dairy Free • Easy

2 tablespoons olive oil

2 onions, sliced

4 carrots, sliced

3 leeks, trimmed and sliced

1 pound white mushrooms

2 garlic cloves, crushed

**1-inch piece fresh ginger, peeled
    and grated**

1 tablespoon ground coriander

1 cup split red lentils

3 cups hot vegetable stock

¼ cup freshly chopped cilantro

salt and ground black pepper

1. Preheat the oven to 350°F. Heat the oil in a flameproof Dutch oven, add the onions, carrots, and leeks, and sauté, stirring, for 5 minutes. Add the mushrooms, garlic, ginger, and ground coriander and sauté for 2–3 minutes.

2. Rinse and drain the lentils, and then stir into the casserole with the hot stock. Season with salt and black pepper and return to a boil. Cover and bake in the oven for 45–50 minutes until the vegetables and lentils are tender. Stir in the chopped cilantro before serving.

Moroccan Chickpea Stew

Preparation Time 10 minutes • Cooking Time 40 minutes • Serves 4 • Per Serving 232 calories,
9g fat (1g saturated), 29g carbohydrates, 600mg sodium • Vegetarian • Dairy Free • Easy

1 red bell pepper, halved and
    seeded
1 green bell pepper, halved and
    seeded
1 yellow bell pepper, halved and
    seeded
2 tablespoons olive oil
1 onion, finely sliced
2 garlic cloves, crushed
1 tablespoon harissa paste

2 tablespoons tomato paste
½ teaspoon ground cumin
1 eggplant, diced
1 (15-ounce) can chickpeas,
    drained and rinsed
2 cups vegetable stock
¼ cup freshly chopped Italian
    parsley, plus a few sprigs to
    garnish
salt and ground black pepper

1. Preheat the broiler and lay the bell peppers, skin side up, on a baking sheet. Broil for around 5 minutes until the skin begins to blister and char. Put the bell peppers into a plastic bag, seal, and put to one side for a few minutes. When cooled a little, peel off the blackened skins and discard. Slice the roasted peppers and put to one side.

2. Heat the oil in a large, heavy skillet over low heat, add the onion, and cook for 5–10 minutes, until soft. Add the garlic, harissa, tomato paste, and cumin and cook for 2 minutes.

3. Add the roasted bell peppers to the pan with the eggplant. Stir everything to coat evenly with the spices and cook for 2 minutes. Add the chickpeas and stock, season well with salt and black pepper, and bring to a boil. Reduce the heat and simmer for 20 minutes.

4. Just before serving, stir the parsley through the chickpea stew. Serve in warmed bowls, garnished with parsley sprigs.

Tomato and Lima Bean Stew

Preparation Time 10 minutes • Cooking Time 50–55 minutes • Serves 4 • Per Serving 286 calories, 8g fat (1g saturated), 41g carbohydrates, 1,800mg sodium • Vegetarian • Dairy Free • Easy

2 tablespoons olive oil
1 onion, finely sliced
2 garlic cloves, finely chopped
2 large leeks, trimmed and sliced
2 (14½-ounce) cans cherry tomatoes or diced tomatoes
2 (15-ounce) cans lima beans, drained and rinsed
⅔ cup hot vegetable stock
1–2 tablespoons balsamic vinegar
salt and ground black pepper

1. Preheat the oven to 350°F. Heat the oil in a Dutch oven over medium heat. Add the onion and garlic and cook for 10 minutes or until golden and soft. Add the leeks and cook, covered, for 5 minutes.

2. Add the tomatoes, beans, and hot stock and season well with salt and black pepper. Bring to a boil. Then cover and bake in the oven for 35–40 minutes, until the sauce has thickened. Remove from the oven, stir in the vinegar, and spoon into warmed bowls.

Butternut Squash Risotto with Hazelnut Butter

Preparation Time 15 minutes • Cooking Time 40 minutes • Serves 4 • Per Serving 706 calories, 50g fat (27g saturated), 51g carbohydrates, 1,100mg sodium • Vegetarian • Gluten Free • Easy

4 tablespoons butter

1 cup finely chopped onion

1 butternut squash, halved, peeled, seeded, and cut into small cubes

2 garlic cloves, crushed

1 cup risotto rice

2½ cups hot chicken stock

grated zest of ½ an orange

½ ounce vegetarian Parmesan (see Cook's Tips), freshly shaved

salt and ground black pepper

FOR THE HAZELNUT BUTTER

⅓ cup hazelnuts

½ cup (1 stick) butter, softened

2 tablespoons freshly chopped Italian parsley

1. To make the hazelnut butter, spread the hazelnuts on a baking sheet and toast under a hot broiler until golden brown, turning frequently. Put the nuts in a clean dish towel and rub off the skins, and then chop finely. Put the nuts, butter, and parsley on a piece of wax paper. Season with black pepper and mix together. Roll into a log shape, twist the paper at both ends to seal, and chill.

2. To make the risotto, melt the butter in a large skillet and sauté the onion until soft but not browned. Add the squash and sauté over low heat for 5–8 minutes, until just beginning to soften. Add the garlic and rice and stir until well mixed. Increase the heat to medium and add the hot stock a little at a time, allowing for the liquid to be absorbed after each addition. This will take about 25 minutes.

3. Stir in the orange zest and Parmesan and season with salt and black pepper. Serve the risotto with a slice of the hazelnut butter melting on top.

COOK'S TIPS

• *You can use other types of squash, such as acorn or kabocha.*

• *Vegetarian cheeses: Some vegetarians prefer to avoid cheeses that have been produced by the traditional method, because this uses animal-derived rennet. Some supermarkets and cheese shops now stock vegetarian cheeses, produced using vegetarian rennet.*

Caramelized Onion and Goat Cheese Tart

Preparation Time 10 minutes • Cooking Time 1 hour • Serves 6 • Per Serving 480 calories, 28g fat (14g saturated), 44g carbohydrates, 1,500mg sodium • Vegetarian • Easy

1 rolled pie crust dough, thawed if frozen

all-purpose flour to dust

10 ounces onion relish from a jar or 3 onions, sliced and sauteed until caramelized

12 ounces mild soft goat cheese

1 large egg, beaten

¼ cup freshly grated Parmesan (see Cook's Tip on page 130)

2 cups arugula

balsamic vinegar and extra virgin olive oil to drizzle

salt and ground black pepper

1. Preheat the oven to 400°F. Roll the pie dough on a lightly floured counter and line an 8-inch diameter, 1-inch deep, loose-bottom fluted tart pan. Prick the pie crust all over with a fork, line the pie crust with parchment paper, fill with pie weights or dried beans, and bake (see Cook's Tip) for 10 minutes. Remove the paper and weights, and bake for another 15–20 minutes, until golden brown.

2. Spoon the onion into the pie crust. Beat the goat cheese and egg together in a bowl until smooth, season with salt and black pepper, and then spoon on top of the onions. Level the surface with a knife and sprinkle the Parmesan over. Bake the tart for 25–30 minutes, until the filling is set and just beginning to turn golden brown.

3. Let cool for 15 minutes. Cut away the sides of the pan and carefully slide the tart onto a plate. Just before serving, arrange the arugula on top of the tart and drizzle with balsamic vinegar and olive oil. Serve warm.

COOK'S TIP

Baking "blind"

Cooking the pie crust before filling it produces a crisp result. Preheat the oven according to the recipe. Prick the bottom of pie crust with a fork. Cover with aluminum foil or parchment paper 3 inches larger than the pan. Spread pie weights or dried beans on top. Bake for 15–20 minutes. Remove the foil or paper and weights and bake for 5–10 minutes, until the pie crust is light golden brown. When cooked and while still hot, brush the bottom of the pie crust with a little beaten egg to seal the fork pricks or any cracks. This will prevent any filling from leaking, which can make it difficult to remove the pie or tart from the pan.

Baked Tomatoes and Fennel

Preparation Time 10 minutes • Cooking Time 1¼ hours • Serves 6 • Per Serving 127 calories,
9g fat (1g saturated), 7g carbohydrates, 100mg sodium • Vegetarian • Gluten Free • Dairy Free • Easy

**4 heads fennel (about 2 pounds),
trimmed and cut into quarters**
⅓ cup white wine*
5 fresh thyme sprigs
⅓ cup olive oil
**6 ripe beefsteak or 16 plum
tomatoes (about 2 pounds)**

1. Preheat the oven to 400°F. Put
the fennel into a roasting pan and
pour the wine over. Snip the thyme
sprigs over the fennel, drizzle with
the oil, and roast for 45 minutes.

2. Halve the tomatoes, add to
the roasting pan, and continue
to roast for 30 minutes or until
tender, basting with the juices
halfway through.

*This recipe is not suitable for
children because it contains
alcohol.*

COOK'S TIP
*This is a delicious accompaniment
to broiled fish or meat, or a
vegetarian frittata.*

Roasted Ratatouille

Preparation Time 15 minutes • Cooking Time 1½ hours • Serves 6 • Per Serving 224 calories, 18g fat (3g saturated), 14g carbohydrates, trace sodium • Vegetarian • Gluten Free • Dairy Free • Easy

4 red bell peppers, seeded and coarsely chopped

1½ large eggplant, cut into chunks

3 onions, cut into wedges

4 or 5 garlic cloves, unpeeled and left whole

⅔ cup olive oil

1 teaspoon fennel seeds

¾ cup canned tomato puree or sauce

sea salt flakes and ground black pepper

a few fresh thyme sprigs to garnish

1. Preheat the oven to 475°F. Put the bell peppers, eggplant, onions, garlic, oil, and fennel seeds into a roasting pan. Season with sea salt flakes and black pepper and toss together.

2. Transfer to the oven and bake for 30 minutes (tossing frequently during cooking) or until the vegetables are charred and beginning to soften.

3. Stir the tomato puree or sauce through the vegetables and put the roasting pan back in the oven for 50–60 minutes, stirring occasionally. Garnish with the thyme sprigs and serve.

TRY SOMETHING DIFFERENT

Replace half the eggplant with 3 zucchini; use a mixture of green and red bell peppers; garnish with fresh basil instead of thyme.

Roasted Vegetable Salad with Mustard Mayonnaise

Preparation Time 15 minutes • Cooking Time 40 minutes • Serves 4 • Per Serving 420 calories, 43g fat (6g saturated), 5g carbohydrates, 1,000mg sodium • Vegetarian • Gluten Free • Dairy Free • Easy

2 pounds mixed vegetables (such as fennel, zucchini, leeks, eggplants, baby turnips, new potatoes, and red onions)
2 garlic cloves, unpeeled
4–5 fresh marjoram or rosemary sprigs
⅓ cup olive oil
1 teaspoon sea salt flakes
mixed crushed peppercorns to taste
4 teaspoons balsamic vinegar
warm crusty bread to serve

FOR THE MUSTARD MAYONNAISE
⅔ cup mayonnaise
2 tablespoons Dijon mustard
salt and ground black pepper

1. Preheat the oven to 425°F. For the vegetables, quarter the fennel, chop the zucchini, leeks, and eggplant, trim the turnips, and cut the onions into petals. Place the vegetables, garlic, marjoram or rosemary, the oil, salt, and peppercorns in a roasting pan and toss well (see Cook's Tip).

2. Roast in the oven for 30–35 minutes or until the vegetables are golden brown, tossing frequently. Sprinkle the vinegar over the top and return to the oven for another 5 minutes.

3. To make the mustard mayonnaise, mix the mayonnaise with the mustard. Season with salt and black pepper and set aside.

4. Arrange the vegetable salad on a serving dish and serve with the mustard mayonnaise and crusty bread.

COOK'S TIP
It's best to roast vegetables in a single layer or they will steam and become soggy. Use two pans if necessary.

Eggplant and Lentil Curry

Preparation Time 10 minutes • Cooking Time 40–45 minutes • Serves 4 • Per Serving 335 calories, 15g fat (3g saturated), 39g carbohydrates, 200mg sodium • Vegetarian • Easy

3 tablespoons olive oil

2 eggplants, cut into 1-inch cubes

1 onion, chopped

2 tablespoons mild curry paste

3 (14½ ounce) cans diced tomatoes

¾ cup hot vegetable stock

1¼ cups red lentils, rinsed

1 cup spinach leaves

½ cup fresh cilantro, roughly chopped

2 tablespoons fat-free Greek yogurt

rice to serve (optional)

1. Heat 2 tablespoons oil in a large skillet over a low heat and fry the eggplant cubes until golden. Remove from the pan and set aside.

2. Heat the remaining oil in the same skillet and fry the onion for 8–10 minutes until soft. Add the curry paste and stir-fry for another 2 minutes.

3. Add the tomatoes, hot stock, lentils, and reserved eggplant to the skillet. Bring to a boil. Then reduce the heat to a low simmer, half-cover the skillet with a lid, and simmer for 25 minutes or according to the lentils package directions.

4. At the end of cooking, stir the spinach, cilantro, and yogurt through the curry. Serve with rice, if desired.

COOK'S TIP

Choose eggplant that are firm, shiny and blemish-free, with a bright green stem.

COMFORT
FOOD

Slow-Braised Garlic Chicken

Preparation Time 30 minutes • Cooking Time about 2 hours • Serves 6 • Per Serving 506 calories, 28g fat (9g saturated), 10g carbohydrates, 1,000mg sodium • A Little Effort

2 tablespoons olive oil

1 tablespoon freshly chopped thyme

2 cups finely chopped cremini mushrooms

6 whole chicken legs (drumsticks and thighs)

18 thin slices pancetta or bacon

2 tablespoons all-purpose flour

2 tablespoons butter

18 small shallots

12 garlic cloves, unpeeled but split

3 cups (1 bottle) full-bodied white wine*, such as Chardonnay

2 bay leaves

salt and ground black pepper

1. Preheat the oven to 350°F. Heat 1 tablespoon oil in a skillet and sauté the thyme and mushrooms until all the moisture has evaporated and the mixture is dry. Season and let cool.

2. Loosen the skin away from one chicken leg and spoon a little of the mushroom paste underneath. Season the leg all over with salt and black pepper, and then wrap three pancetta slices around the thigh end. Repeat with the remaining chicken legs, and dust using 1 tablespoon flour.

3. Melt the butter in a skillet with the remaining oil over high heat. Cook the chicken legs, in batches of two, seam side down, until browned. Turn the legs, brown the other side, and transfer to a deep Dutch oven. The browning process should take about 8–10 minutes per batch.

4. Put the shallots and garlic into the skillet and cook for 10 minutes or until browned. Sprinkle the remaining flour over them and cook for 1 minute. Pour in the wine and bring to a boil, stirring. Pour into the Dutch oven with the chicken and add the bay leaves. Cover and bake in the oven for 1½ hours. Serve hot.

* This recipe is not suitable for children because it contains alcohol.

GET AHEAD

To prepare ahead *Complete the recipe to the end of step 4. Cool quickly, and freeze in an airtight container for up to one month.*
To use *Thaw overnight at cool room temperature. Preheat the oven to 425°F. Put the chicken back into the casserole and reheat in the oven for 15 minutes. Reduce the oven temperature to 350°F and cook for another 25 minutes.*

Braised Beef with Mustard and Capers

Preparation Time 15 minutes • Cooking Time 2 hours 20 minutes, plus cooling • Serves 4 • Per Serving 391 calories, 19g fat (7g saturated), 10g carbohydrates, 1,500mg sodium • Gluten Free • Dairy Free • Easy

1 (2-ounce) can anchovy fillets in oil, drained, chopped, and oil put to one side
about 2 tablespoons olive oil
1½ pounds chuck shoulder steak, cut into small strips
¼ cup cold water
2 large Spanish onions, peeled and thinly sliced
2 tablespoons capers
1 teaspoon English mustard
6 fresh thyme sprigs
½ cup freshly chopped Italian parsley
salt and ground black pepper
green salad and crusty bread or mashed potatoes to serve

1. Preheat the oven to 325°F. Measure the anchovy oil into a deep flameproof casserole, and then make up to 3 tablespoons with the olive oil. Heat the oil and sauté the meat, a few pieces at a time, until well browned. Remove with a slotted spoon and set aside. Pour the cold water into the empty casserole and stir to loosen any sediment on the bottom.

2. Put the meat back into the dish and add the onions, anchovies, capers, mustard, half the thyme, and all but 1 tablespoon of the parsley. Stir until thoroughly mixed.

3. Tear off a sheet of parchment paper big enough to cover the pan. Crumple it up and wet it under cold running water. Squeeze out most of the water, spread it out, and press down over the surface of the meat.

4. Cover with a tight-fitting lid and cook in the oven for 2 hours or until the beef is meltingly tender. Check the casserole after 1 hour to make sure it's still moist. If it looks dry, add a little water.

5. Adjust for seasoning and stir in the remaining parsley and thyme. Serve with a green salad and crusty bread or mashed potatoes.

COOK'S TIP
To make deliciously easy mashed potatoes, put four russet potatoes in the oven when you put in the casserole. Let bake for 2 hours. Cut each potato in half and use a fork to scrape out the flesh into a bowl. Add 4 tablespoons butter and season well with salt and black pepper—the potato will be soft enough to mash with a fork.

Braised Lamb Shanks

Preparation Time 20–25 minutes • Cooking Time 2¾ hours • Serves 6 • Per Serving 355 calories, 16g fat (6g saturated), 23g carbohydrates, 1,200mg sodium • Gluten Free • Dairy Free • Easy

6 small lamb shanks

1 pound shallots, peeled but left whole

2 medium eggplants, cut into small dice

2 tablespoons olive oil

3 tablespoons harissa paste

pared zest of 1 orange and juice of 3 large oranges

¾ cup medium sherry*

3 cups canned tomato puree or tomato sauce

1¼ cups hot vegetable or lamb stock

½ cup dried apricots

½ cup cherries (optional)

a large pinch of saffron threads

couscous and green beans to serve (optional)

1. Preheat the oven to 350°F. Heat a large Dutch oven over medium heat and brown the lamb shanks all over. Allow 10–12 minutes to do this—the better the color now, the better the flavor of the finished dish.

2. Remove the lamb and put to one side. Add the shallots, eggplants, and oil to the pot and cook over high heat, stirring from time to time, until the shallots and eggplants are golden and beginning to soften.

3. Reduce the heat and add the lamb and all the other ingredients except the couscous and beans. The liquid should come halfway up the shanks. Bring to a boil. Then cover tightly and bake in the oven for 2½ hours. Test the lamb with a fork—it should be so tender that it almost falls off the bone.

4. If the cooking liquid looks too thin, remove the lamb to a heated serving plate, and then simmer the sauce on the stove until reduced and thickened. Put the lamb back into the pot. Serve with couscous and green beans, if desired.

* This recipe is not suitable for children because it contains alcohol.

COOK'S TIP
Cooking lamb shanks in a rich sauce in the oven at a low temperature makes the meat meltingly tender.

Moroccan Lamb Stew

Preparation Time 20 minutes • Cooking Time about 1 hour 20 minutes, plus standing • Serves 6 •
Per Serving 274 calories, 11g fat (5g saturated), 25g carbohydrates, 200mg sodium • Dairy Free • Easy

**1 pound lamb shoulder, well
trimmed to remove excess fat,
and then coarsely cubed**
2 tablespoons all-purpose flour
½ tablespoon sunflower oil
1 onion, thickly sliced
2 carrots, coarsely chopped
2 garlic cloves, crushed
2 teaspoons harissa paste
1 teaspoon ground cinnamon
2 (14½-ounce) cans diced tomatoes
**½ cup dried apricots, coarsely
chopped**
½ cup couscous
**a large handful of fresh curly
parsley, coarsely chopped**
salt and ground black pepper

1. Dust the lamb with the flour. Heat the oil in a large saucepan and brown the lamb in batches. Set aside. In the same pan, add the onions and carrots, and gently sauté for 10 minutes. Add a splash of water if they start to stick to the pan.

2. Stir in the garlic, harissa, and cinnamon and cook for 1 minute. Add a splash of water and use a wooden spoon to help scrape any sediment from the bottom of the pan, and then stir it in. Pour in the tomatoes and return the lamb to the pan. Stir in the apricots and season. Cover and simmer for 1 hour or until the lamb is tender. Season to taste.

3. Meanwhile, put the couscous into a bowl and add boiling water according to the package directions. Cover with plastic wrap and let stand for 10 minutes. When ready, fluff up the grains with a fork and stir in the parsley. Season. Serve the lamb topped with spoonfuls of couscous (see Cook's Tip).

COOK'S TIP
Watching your carb intake? Serving the couscous as a garnish on the stew instead of as a substantial side dish is a satisfying alternative.

Lamb and Bamboo Shoot Red Curry

Preparation Time 10 minutes • Cooking Time 45 minutes • Serves 4 • Per Serving 397 calories, 25g fat (8g saturated), 17g carbohydrates, 400mg sodium • Gluten Free • Dairy Free • Easy

2 tablespoons sunflower oil

1 large onion, cut into wedges

2 garlic cloves, finely chopped

1 pound lean boneless lamb, cut into 1¼-inch cubes

2 tablespoons Thai red curry paste

⅔ cup lamb or beef stock

2 tablespoons Thai fish sauce

2 teaspoons packed light brown sugar

1 (7-ounce) can bamboo shoots, drained and thinly sliced

1 red bell pepper, seeded and thinly sliced

2 tablespoons freshly chopped mint

1 tablespoon freshly chopped basil

¼ cup unsalted peanuts, toasted rice to serve

1. Heat the oil in a wok or large skillet, add the onion and garlic, and sauté over medium heat for 5 minutes.

2. Add the lamb and the curry paste and stir-fry for 5 minutes. Add the stock, fish sauce, and sugar and bring to a boil. Reduce the heat, cover the pan, and simmer gently for 20 minutes.

3. Stir the bamboo shoots, red bell pepper, and herbs into the curry and cook, uncovered, for another 10 minutes. Stir in the peanuts and serve immediately, with rice.

Spicy Beans with Jazzed-up Potatoes

Preparation Time 12 minutes • Cooking Time about 1½ hours • Serves 4 • Per Serving 298 calories,
4g fat (1g saturated), 56g carbohydrates, 800mg sodium • Vegetarian • Gluten Free • Easy

4 baking potatoes
1 tablespoon olive oil, plus extra
to rub
1 teaspoon smoked paprika, plus
a pinch
2 shallots, finely chopped
1 tablespoon freshly chopped
rosemary
1 (14½-ounce) can cannellini
beans, drained and rinsed
1 (14½-ounce) can diced tomatoes

1 tablespoon packed light brown
sugar
1 teaspoon Worcestershire sauce
⅓ cup red wine*
⅓ cup hot vegetable stock
a small handful of freshly chopped
Italian parsley
grated mature cheddar (see Cook's
Tip on page 130), to sprinkle
sea salt and ground black pepper

1. Preheat the oven to 400°F. Rub
the potatoes with a little oil and put
them on a baking tray. Scatter with
sea salt and a pinch of smoked
paprika. Bake for 1–1½ hours.

2. Meanwhile, heat 1 tablespoon
oil in a large pan, and then sauté
the shallots over low heat for 1–2
minutes until they start to soften.

3. Add the rosemary and
1 teaspoon paprika and fry for
1–2 minutes. Add the beans,
tomatoes, sugar, Worcestershire
sauce, wine, and hot stock. Season,
bring to a boil, and then simmer,
uncovered, for 10–15 minutes.
Serve the baked potatoes with
beans on top, sprinkled with parsley
and grated cheddar.

* This recipe is not suitable for
children because it contains
alcohol.

TRY SOMETHING
DIFFERENT
For a quick meal that takes less than
25 minutes, the spicy beans are just
as good served with toast.

Squid and Vegetables in Black Bean Sauce

Preparation Time 35 minutes • Cooking Time 10–15 minutes • Serves 4 • Per Serving 274 calories, 15g fat (2g saturated), 12g carbohydrates, 1,000mg sodium • Gluten Free • Dairy Free • A Little Effort

1 pound squid, cleaned
2 tablespoons sesame seeds
2 tablespoons sunflower oil
1 tablespoon sesame oil
2 garlic cloves
2 dried red chilies
¾ cup broccoli florets
1 cup trimmed snow peas
1 carrot, thinly sliced
⅔ cup small cauliflower florets
1 small green or red bell pepper, seeded and thinly sliced
¾ cup shredded napa cabbage or bok choy
¼ cup bean sprouts
2 tablespoons freshly chopped cilantro

FOR THE SAUCE
2 tablespoons black bean sauce
1 tablespoon Thai fish sauce
2–3 teaspoons honey
⅓ cup fish or vegetable stock
1 tablespoon tamarind juice
2 teaspoons cornstarch

1. First, prepare the sauce. Mix all ingredients together in a small bowl and whisk until smooth.

2. Wash and dry the squid and halve the tentacles if large. Open out the body pouches, score diagonally, and cut into large squares. Set aside.

3. Toast the sesame seeds in a dry wok or large skillet over medium heat, stirring until they turn golden brown. Transfer to a plate.

4. Heat the sunflower and sesame oils in the same pan. Add the garlic and chilies and sauté gently for 5 minutes. Remove the garlic and chilies with a slotted spoon and discard.

5. Add all the vegetables to the pan and stir-fry for 3 minutes. Add the squid, increase the heat, and stir-fry for another 2 minutes or until the squid curls up and turns opaque. Add the sauce and let simmer for 1 minute.

6. Sprinkle the sesame seeds and cilantro over the squid and serve immediately.

TRY SOMETHING DIFFERENT
Instead of squid, try 1 pound top sirloin steak, cut into thin strips.

Hash Browns with Fried Eggs

Preparation Time 20 minutes, plus cooling • Cooking Time 20–25 minutes • Serves 4 • Per Serving 324 calories, 16g fat (7g saturated), 36g carbohydrates, 400mg sodium • Gluten Free • Easy

8 russet potatoes (about 2 pounds), scrubbed and left whole
3 tablespoons butter
4 extra-large eggs
salt and ground black pepper
sprigs of fresh Italian parsley to garnish

1. Put the potatoes into a large saucepan of cold water. Cover, bring to a boil, and parboil for 5–8 minutes. Drain and let cool for 15 minutes.

2. Preheat the oven to 300°F. Put a baking sheet inside to warm. Peel the potatoes and coarsely shred them lengthwise into long strands. Divide into eight portions and shape into mounds.

3. Melt half the butter in a large nonstick skillet. When it is beginning to brown, add four of the potato mounds, spacing them well apart, and flatten them a little. Pan-fry slowly for 6–7 minutes, until golden brown. Turn them and brown the other side for 6–7 minutes. Transfer to the warmed baking sheet and keep warm in the oven while you pan-fry the rest.

4. Just before serving, carefully break the eggs into the hot skillet and cook for about 2 minutes, until the white is set and the yolk is still soft. Season with salt and black pepper and serve at once, with the hash browns. Garnish with sprigs of parsley.

Stuffed Pasta Shells

Preparation Time 15 minutes • Cooking Time about 1 hour • Serves 6 • Per Serving 378 calories,
17g fat (5g saturated), 41g carbohydrates, 1,100mg sodium • Easy

2 tablespoons olive oil

1 large onion, finely chopped

**a few fresh rosemary or oregano
  sprigs, chopped**

**4 ounces small, flat mushrooms,
  sliced**

**6 plump Italian-style link sausages,
  skinned**

¾ cup red wine*

**1¼ cups tomato puree or tomato
  sauce**

¼ cup tomato paste

sugar to taste, if necessary

**8 ounces large pasta shells, such as
  conchiglioni rigati**

**⅔ cup reduced-fat light cream
  (optional)**

freshly grated Parmesan to garnish

green salad to serve

1. Preheat the oven to 350°F. Heat
the oil in a deep skillet. Stir in the
onion and rosemary or oregano and
cook over gentle heat for 10 minutes
or until the onion is soft and golden
brown. Add the mushrooms and
cook over medium heat until the
vegetables are soft and beginning
to brown at the edges. Transfer the
onion mixture to a bowl.

2. Crumble the sausage meat into
the hot pan and stir over high heat
with a wooden spoon, breaking the
meat up as you do so, until browned
all over. Reduce the heat slightly and
pour in the wine. Let simmer and
reduce by about half. Return the
onion mixture to the pan and add the
tomato puree or sauce and tomato
paste. Simmer gently for another
10 minutes. Add a pinch of sugar if
the sauce tastes a little sharp.

3. While the sauce is simmering,
cook the pasta shells in plenty of
boiling water according to the
package directions until just tender.
Drain well and run under cold water
to cool.

4. Fill the shells with the sauce and
put into a shallow ovenproof dish.
Drizzle with any extra sauce and
the cream, if using, and bake for
30 minutes or until piping hot.
Sprinkle with Parmesan and serve
with a big bowl of green salad.

** This recipe is not suitable for
children because it contains
alcohol.*

**TRY SOMETHING
DIFFERENT**

*• Ground turkey or chicken would
make a lighter alternative to the
sausages; you will need 1 pound.*

*• Use a small eggplant, diced,
instead of the mushrooms.*

Cannelloni with Roasted Garlic

Preparation Time 40 minutes • Cooking Time about 1 hour • Serves 6 • Per serving 430 calories, 20g fat (9g saturated), 29g carbohydrates, trace sodium • A Little Effort

20 garlic cloves, unpeeled
2 tablespoons extra virgin olive oil
½ ounce dried porcini mushrooms,
    soaked for 20 minutes in ⅔ cup
    boiling water
5 shallots or pearl onions,
    finely chopped
1½ pounds ground round or
    ground sirloin beef
¾ cup beef or lamb stock
2 tablespoons freshly chopped
    thyme
about 12 fresh egg lasagna noodles
½ cup light cream mixed with
    2 tablespoons tomato paste
butter to grease
⅔ cup shredded Gruyère cheese
    (see Cook's Tip on page 130)
salt and ground black pepper

1. Preheat the oven to 350°F. Put the garlic into a small roasting pan with 1 tablespoon oil. Toss to coat the garlic in the oil and bake for 25 minutes or until soft. Let cool.

2. Meanwhile, drain the porcini mushrooms, putting the liquid to one side. Rinse to remove any grit. Finely chop the mushrooms.

3. Heat the remaining oil in a saucepan. Add the shallots and cook over medium heat for 5 minutes or until soft. Increase the heat and stir in the meat. Cook, stirring frequently, until browned. Add the stock, the mushrooms, with their liquid, and the thyme. Cook over medium heat for 15–20 minutes, until the liquid has almost evaporated. The mixture should be moist. Peel the garlic cloves and mash them to a coarse paste with a fork. Stir into the meat mixture, and then season with salt and black pepper and set aside.

4. Cook the lasagna according to the package directions until al dente. Drain, rinse with cold water, and drain again. Lay each lasagna noodle on a clean dish towel. Spoon the meat mixture along one long edge, and then roll up to enclose the filling. Cut the tubes in half.

5. Season the cream and tomato paste mixture. Preheat the oven to 400°F. Grease a shallow baking dish. Arrange a layer of filled tubes in the bottom of the dish. Spoon half the tomato cream over them and sprinkle with half the cheese. Arrange the remaining tubes on top and cover with the remaining tomato cream and cheese. Cover the dish with aluminum foil and cook in the oven for 10 minutes. Uncover and cook for another 5–10 minutes until lightly browned, and then serve.

Mushroom Cannelloni

Preparation Time 15 minutes • Cooking Time 50–55 minutes • Serves 4 • Per Serving 631 calories, 37g fat (18g saturated), 50g carbohydrates, 1,900mg sodium • A Little Effort

6 fresh egg lasagna noodles
3 tablespoons olive oil
1 small onion, finely sliced
3 garlic cloves, sliced
¼ cup freshly chopped thyme
8 ounces cremini or brown-cap mushrooms, coarsely chopped
4 ounces flat-cap mushrooms, coarsely chopped
2 (4-ounce) goat cheese logs, with rind
1½ cups ready-made cheesy white sauce (see Cook's Tip on page 64)
salt and ground black pepper

1. Preheat the oven to 350°F. Cook the lasagna noodles according to the package directions. Drain, rinse with cold water, and drain again. Keep covered with cold water until ready to use.

2. Heat the oil in a large saucepan and add the onion. Cook over medium heat for 7–10 minutes, until the onion is soft. Add the garlic and sauté for 1–2 minutes. Keep a few slices of garlic to one side. Keep a little thyme for sprinkling later, and add the rest to the pan with the mushrooms. Cook for another 5 minutes or until the mushrooms are golden brown and there is no excess liquid in the pan. Season, remove from the heat, and put to one side.

3. Crumble one of the goat cheese logs into the cooled mushroom mixture and stir together. Drain the lasagna noodles and pat dry with paper towels. Spoon 2–3 tablespoons of the mushroom mixture along the long edge of each lasagna noodle, leaving a ½-inch border. Roll up the pasta noodles and cut each roll in half. Put the pasta into a shallow ovenproof dish and spoon the cheese sauce over it. Slice the remaining goat cheese into thick circles and arrange across the middle of the pasta rolls. Sprinkle the reserved garlic and thyme on top. Bake in the oven for 30–35 minutes until golden brown and bubbling.

COOK'S TIP
Fresh egg lasagna noodles wrapped around a filling are used here to make cannelloni, but you can also buy cannelloni tubes, which can easily be filled using a teaspoon.

Spaghetti with a Spicy Meat Sauce

Preparation Time 15 minutes • Cooking Time 30–40 minutes • Serves 4 • Per Serving 756 calories, 33g fat (13g saturated), 74g carbohydrates, 1,400mg sodium • Easy

1 tablespoon olive oil

1 large onion, finely chopped

½ large red chili, seeded and thinly sliced (see Cook's Tip on page 15)

1 pound ground round or ground sirloin beef

4 ounces smoked bacon, rind removed, cut into strips

3 roasted red peppers, drained and finely chopped

1 (14½-ounce) can diced tomatoes

½ cup red wine*

12 ounces spaghetti

¼ cup shredded cheddar or Gruyère cheese, plus extra to garnish

2 tablespoons freshly chopped Italian parsley (optional), plus extra to garnish

salt and ground black pepper

1. Heat the oil in a large saucepan over medium heat. Add the onion and chili and sauté for 5–10 minutes, until soft and golden brown. Add the beef and the bacon strips, and stir over the heat for 5–7 minutes until well browned.

2. Stir in the red peppers, tomatoes, and wine. Season with salt and black pepper and bring to a boil, and then reduce the heat and simmer over low heat for 15–20 minutes.

3. Meanwhile, cook the pasta in a large saucepan of lightly salted boiling water according to the package directions. Drain.

4. Just before serving, stir the shredded cheese, parsley, if using, and the sauce into the spaghetti. Garnish with extra grated cheese and chopped parsley.

* This recipe is not suitable for children because it contains alcohol.

TRY SOMETHING DIFFERENT

Ground lamb would make a tasty alternative to the beef; you will need 1 pound.

Italian Meatballs

Preparation Time 15 minutes • Cooking Time 50 minutes • Serves 4 • Per Serving 275 calories, 12g fat (4g saturated), 16g carbohydrates, 1,800mg sodium • Dairy Free • Easy

1 cup fresh bread crumbs
1 pound ground lean pork
1 teaspoon fennel seeds, crushed
¼ teaspoon dried red pepper
   flakes, or to taste
3 garlic cloves, crushed
¼ cup freshly chopped Italian
   parsley
3 tablespoons red wine*
oil-water spray (see Cook's Tip)
freshly chopped oregano
   to garnish
spaghetti to serve

FOR THE TOMATO SAUCE
oil-water spray
2 large shallots, finely chopped
3 ripe black olives, pitted and
   shredded
2 garlic cloves, crushed
2 pinches of dried red pepper
   flakes
1 cup vegetable or chicken stock
2 cups tomato puree or tomato
   sauce
2 tablespoons each freshly
   chopped Italian parsley, basil,
   and oregano
salt and ground black pepper

1. To make the tomato sauce, spray a saucepan with the oil-water spray and add the shallots. Cook gently for 5 minutes. Add the olives, garlic, red pepper flakes, and stock and bring to a boil. Reduce the heat, cover, and simmer for 3–4 minutes.

2. Uncover and simmer for 10 minutes or until the shallots and garlic are soft and the liquid syrupy. Stir in the tomato puree or sauce and season with salt and black pepper. Bring to a boil, and then reduce the heat and simmer for 10–15 minutes. Stir in the herbs.

3. Meanwhile, put the bread crumbs, pork, fennel seeds, red pepper flakes, garlic, parsley, and wine into a large bowl, season, and mix together, using your hands, until thoroughly combined. (If you want to check the seasoning, sauté a little mixture, taste, and adjust, if necessary.)

4. With wet hands, roll the mixture into balls. Line a broiler pan with aluminum foil, shiny side up, and spray with the oil-water spray. Cook the meatballs under a preheated broiler for 3–4 minutes on each side. Serve with the tomato sauce and spaghetti, garnished with oregano.

* This recipe is not suitable for children because it contains alcohol.

COOK'S TIP

Oil-water spray is far lower in calories than oil alone and, because it sprays on thinly and evenly, you'll use less. Fill one-eighth of a travel-size spray bottle with oil such as sunflower, light olive, or vegetable oil, and then fill up with water. To use, shake well before spraying. Store in the refrigerator.

Greek Pasta Bake

Preparation Time 10 minutes • Cooking Time about 1½ hours • Serves 4 • Per Serving 736 calories, 30g fat (13g saturated), 80g carbohydrates, 800mg sodium • Easy

2 tablespoons vegetable oil
1 onion, finely chopped
2 garlic cloves, crushed
1 pound extra-lean ground lamb
2 tablespoons tomato paste
1 (14½-ounce) can diced tomatoes
2 bay leaves
⅔ cup hot beef stock
12 ounces macaroni
½ cup shredded cheddar
salt and ground black pepper

FOR THE SAUCE
1 tablespoon butter
2 tablespoons all-purpose flour
1¼ cups milk
1 large egg, beaten

1. Heat the oil in a large saucepan, add the onion and garlic, and cook for 5 minutes to soften. Add the lamb and stir-fry over high heat for 3–4 minutes, until browned all over.

2. Stir in the tomato paste and cook for 1–2 minutes. Stir in the tomatoes, bay leaves, and hot stock, and season with salt and black pepper. Bring to a boil, and then reduce the heat and cook for 35–40 minutes.

3. Meanwhile, make the sauce. Melt the butter in a small saucepan, and then stir in the flour and cook over medium heat for 1–2 minutes. Gradually add the milk, stirring constantly. Reduce the heat to low and cook, stirring, for 4–5 minutes. Remove from the heat and cool slightly. Stir in the beaten egg and season well with salt and black pepper. Put to one side.

4. Preheat the oven to 350°F. Cook the macaroni in a large saucepan of lightly salted boiling water according to the package directions until al dente.

5. Drain the pasta well and spoon half into a 2-quart ovenproof dish. Spoon the meat mixture over it. Top with the remaining macaroni. Pour the sauce evenly over the top and sprinkle with the shredded cheese. Bake in the oven for 25–30 minutes, until golden brown.

Classic Lasagna

Preparation Time about 1 hour • Cooking Time 1 hour 20 minutes, plus standing • Serves 6 • Per Serving 326 calories, 13g fat (6g saturated), 37g carbohydrates, 500mg sodium • Easy

butter to grease
12–15 fresh egg lasagna noodles or
    oven-ready lasagna noodles (see
    Cook's Tip)
3 tablespoons freshly grated
    Parmesan
salad to serve

FOR THE MEAT SAUCE
2 tablespoons olive oil
1 onion, finely chopped
2 garlic cloves, crushed
1 pound ground round or ground
    sirloin beef
2 tablespoons tomato paste
1¼ cups red wine*
1 (14½-ounce) can diced tomatoes
4 ounces cremini mushrooms,
    sliced
2 tablespoons Worcestershire sauce
salt and ground black pepper

FOR THE WHITE SAUCE
1¼ cups low-fat milk
1 onion slice
6 peppercorns
1 mace blade
1 bay leaf
1 tablespoon butter
2 tablespoons all-purpose flour
freshly grated nutmeg
salt and ground black pepper

1. To make the meat sauce, heat the oil in a large saucepan, add the onion, and sauté over medium heat for 10 minutes or until softened and golden brown. Add the garlic and cook for 1 minute. Add the beef and brown evenly, using a wooden spoon to break up the pieces. Stir in the tomato paste and wine, cover, and bring to a boil. Add the tomatoes, mushrooms, and Worcestershire sauce and season well with salt and black pepper. Bring back to a boil, reduce the heat, and simmer for 20 minutes.

2. Meanwhile, to make the white (béchamel) sauce, pour the milk into a saucepan and add the onion, peppercorns, mace, and bay leaf. Bring almost to a boil. Remove from the heat, cover, and let stand for about 20 minutes to let the flavors develop. Strain. Melt the butter in a saucepan, add the flour slowly, and cook, stirring, for 1 minute or until cooked but not browned. Remove from the heat and gradually pour in the milk, whisking constantly. Season lightly with nutmeg, salt, and black pepper. Return to the heat and cook, stirring constantly, until the sauce is thickened and smooth. Simmer gently for 2 minutes.

3. Preheat the oven to 350°F. Spoon one-third of the meat sauce over the bottom of a greased 2-quart ovenproof dish. Cover with a layer of lasagna noodles, and then a layer of white sauce. Repeat these layers twice again, finishing with a layer of white sauce to cover the pasta.

4. Sprinkle the Parmesan over the top and stand the dish on a baking sheet. Bake in the oven for 45 minutes or until well browned and bubbling. Serve with salad.

* This recipe is not suitable for children because it contains alcohol.

COOK'S TIP
If using oven-ready lasagna noodles, add a little extra stock or water to the sauce.

Saffron Risotto with Lemon Chicken

Preparation Time 20 minutes • Cooking Time 50 minutes • Serves 4 • Per Serving 830 calories, 44g fat (15g saturated), 50g carbohydrates, 900mg sodium • Gluten Free • Easy

zest and juice of 1 lemon
a small handful of fresh parsley
1¼ cups blanched almonds
1 tablespoon dried thyme
1 garlic clove
⅓ cup olive oil
2 cups hot chicken stock
4 boneless chicken breasts, skin on
4 tablespoons butter
2 onions, finely chopped
a small pinch of saffron threads
1 cup risotto rice
½ cup white wine*
½ cup freshly grated Parmesan
salt and ground black pepper
fresh thyme sprigs to garnish
lemon wedges to serve

1. Preheat the oven to 400°F. Blend the lemon zest, parsley, almonds, thyme, and garlic in a food processor for a few seconds, and then slowly add the oil and process until combined. Season with salt and black pepper. Keep the hot stock at a gentle simmer.

2. Spread the lemon and herb mixture under the skin of the chicken. Put the chicken into a roasting pan. Melt 2 tablespoons butter, brush it over the chicken, and the pour over the lemon juice. Bake in the oven for 25 minutes, basting occasionally.

3. Heat the remaining butter in a saucepan. Add the onions and sauté until soft. Stir in the saffron and rice. Add the wine and a ladleful of the hot stock to the rice and simmer, stirring, until absorbed. Continue adding the stock, a ladleful at a time until the rice is al dente; this will take about 25 minutes. Remove the pan from the heat and stir in the Parmesan. Serve the risotto with the chicken, pouring any juices from the roasting pan over it. Garnish with thyme sprigs and serve with lemon wedges.

* This recipe is not suitable for children because it contains alcohol.

Classic Paella

Preparation Time 15 minutes, plus infusing • Cooking Time 50 minutes • Serves 6 • Per Serving 554 calories, 16g fat (3g saturated), 58g carbohydrates, 500mg sodium • Dairy Free • A Little Effort

4 cups chicken stock

½ teaspoon saffron threads

6 boneless, skinless chicken thighs

⅓ cup extra virgin olive oil

1 large onion, chopped

4 large garlic cloves, crushed

1 teaspoon paprika

2 red bell peppers, seeded and
    sliced

1 (14½-ounce) can diced tomatoes

1¾ cups long-grain rice

¾ cup dry sherry*

1 pound cooked mussels

8 ounces cooked jumbo shrimp

juice of ½ lemon

salt and ground black pepper

lemon wedges and fresh Italian
    parsley to serve

1. Heat the stock in a saucepan, add the saffron, and let steep for 30 minutes. Meanwhile, cut each chicken thigh into three pieces.

2. Heat half the oil in a large skillet and, working in batches, cook the chicken for 3–5 minutes, until pale golden brown on all sides. Set the chicken aside.

3. Reduce the heat slightly and add the remaining oil. Sauté the onion for 5 minutes or until soft. Add the garlic and paprika and stir for 1 minute. Add the chicken, red bell peppers, and tomatoes.

4. Stir in the rice, and then add one-third of the stock and bring to a boil. Season with salt and black pepper.

5. Reduce the heat to a simmer. Cook, uncovered, stirring continuously, until most of the liquid is absorbed.

6. Add the remaining stock a little at a time, letting it become absorbed into the rice before adding more; this should take about 25 minutes. Add the sherry and continue cooking for another 2 minutes; the rice should be wet, because it will continue to absorb liquid.

7. Add the mussels and shrimp to the pan, including all their juices, with the lemon juice. Stir them in and cook for 5 minutes to heat through. Adjust the seasoning, and then garnish with lemon wedges and fresh parsley and serve.

This recipe is not suitable for children because it contains alcohol.

Irish Stew

Preparation Time 15 minutes • Cooking Time 2 hours • Serves 4 • Per Serving 419 calories, 20g fat (9g saturated), 24g carbohydrates, 600mg sodium • Dairy Free • Easy

1½ **pounds lamb cutlets, fat trimmed**

2 **onions, thinly sliced**

4 **red-skinned or white round potatoes, thinly sliced**

1 **tablespoon freshly chopped parsley, plus extra to garnish**

1 **tablespoon dried thyme**

1¼ **cups lamb stock**

salt and ground black pepper

1. Preheat the oven to 325°F. Layer the meat, onions, and potatoes in a deep casserole, sprinkling some herbs and seasoning between each layer. Finish with a layer of potato, overlapping the slices neatly.

2. Pour the stock over the potatoes and cover with parchment paper and a lid. Cook in the oven for 2 hours or until the meat is tender.

3. Preheat the broiler. Take the lid off the casserole and remove the paper. Put the casserole under the broiler and cook until the potatoes have crisped and turned golden brown. Sprinkle with parsley and serve the stew immediately.

Thai Red Turkey Curry

Preparation Time 20 minutes • Cooking Time 18–25 minutes • Serves 6 • Per Serving 248 calories, 8g fat (1g saturated), 16g carbohydrates, 1,200mg sodium • Gluten Free • Dairy Free • Easy

3 tablespoons vegetable oil

3 onions, finely chopped

7 ounces green beans, trimmed

8 baby corn, cut on the diagonal

2 red bell peppers, seeded and cut into thick strips

1 tablespoon Thai red curry paste, or to taste

1 red chili, seeded and finely chopped (see Cook's Tip on page 15)

1 lemongrass stalk, trimmed and finely chopped

4 kaffir lime leaves, bruised

2 tablespoons fresh ginger, peeled and finely chopped

1 garlic clove, crushed

1¾ cups coconut milk

2½ cups chicken or turkey stock

1 pound cooked turkey, cut into strips

1½ cups bean sprouts

fresh basil leaves to garnish

1. Heat the oil in a wok or large skillet, add the onions, and cook for 4–5 minutes or until soft.

2. Add the beans, baby corn, and bell peppers to the pan and stir-fry for 3–4 minutes. Add the curry paste, chili, lemongrass, kaffir lime leaves, ginger, and garlic and cook for another 2 minutes, stirring. Remove from the pan and set aside.

3. Add the coconut milk and stock to the pan, bring to a boil, and simmer vigorously for 5–10 minutes until reduced by one-quarter. Return the vegetables to the pan with the turkey and bean sprouts. Bring to a boil, and then reduce the heat and simmer for 1–2 minutes, until heated through. Garnish with basil leaves and serve immediately.

COOK'S TIP

This is a great way to use up leftover turkey.

Prosciutto and Artichoke Tagliatelle

Preparation Time 5 minutes • Cooking Time 12 minutes • Serves 4 • Per Serving 972 calories,
56g fat (36g saturated), 97g carbohydrates, 1,100mg sodium • Easy

1 pound tagliatelle
2 cups crème fraîche or heavy
   cream
12 roasted artichoke hearts from a
   jar, drained and each cut in half
6 slices prosciutto, torn into strips
2 tablespoons freshly chopped sage
   leaves, plus extra to garnish
salt and ground black pepper
1½ ounces Parmesan shavings to
   serve (see Cook's Tip)

1. Cook the pasta in a large saucepan of lightly salted boiling water according to the package directions.

2. Drain the pasta well, leaving a ladleful of the cooking water in the pan, and then put the pasta back into the pan.

3. Add the crème fraîche or cream to the pan with the artichoke hearts, prosciutto, and sage, and then stir everything together. Season well.

4. Spoon the pasta into warmed bowls, sprinkle with the Parmesan shavings, and garnish with sage. Serve immediately.

COOK'S TIP

Make Parmesan shavings with a vegetable peeler. Hold the piece of cheese in one hand, and pare off wafer-thin strips of cheese using the peeler.

SLOW COOKER SPECIALS

Mexican Bean Soup

Preparation Time 15 minutes • Cooking Time 2–3 hours on high • Serves 6 • Per Serving (without lime butter)
184 calories, 8g fat (1g saturated), 21g carbohydrates, 1,300mg sodium • Vegetarian • Dairy Free • Easy

¼ cup olive oil

1 onion, chopped

2 garlic cloves, chopped

pinch of crushed red pepper flakes

1 teaspoon ground coriander

1 teaspoon ground cumin

½ teaspoon ground cinnamon

2½ cups hot vegetable stock

1¼ cups tomato juice

1–2 teaspoons chili sauce

2 (15-ounce) cans red kidney
   beans, drained and rinsed

2 tablespoons freshly chopped
   cilantro

salt and ground black pepper

fresh cilantro leaves, coarsely torn,
   to garnish

lime butter to serve (optional, see
   Cook's Tip)

1. Heat the oil in a large saucepan, add the onion, garlic, red pepper flakes, and spices, and sauté gently for 5 minutes or until lightly golden brown.

2. Add the hot stock, tomato juice, chili sauce, and beans and bring to a boil, and then transfer to the slow cooker, cover, and cook on high for 2–3 hours.

3. Let the soup sit to cool a little. Process in batches in a blender or food processor until smooth. Pour the soup into a saucepan, stir in the chopped cilantro, and heat through. Season to taste with salt and black pepper.

4. Ladle the soup into warmed bowls. Top each portion with a few slices of lime butter, if desired, and sprinkle with torn cilantro leaves.

COOK'S TIP

Lime Butter

Beat the grated zest and juice of ½ lime into 4 tablespoons softened butter and season to taste with salt and black pepper. Shape into a log, wrap in plastic wrap, and chill until needed. When ready to serve, unwrap and slice thinly.

Split Pea and Ham Soup

Preparation Time 15 minutes, plus overnight soaking • Cooking Time 3–4 hours on high • Serves 6 •
Per Serving 400 calories, 10g fat (5g saturated), 53g carbohydrates, 1,500mg sodium • Gluten Free • Easy

2½ cups dried yellow split peas,
   soaked overnight (see Cook's Tip)
2 tablespoons butter
1 large onion, finely chopped
4 ounces rindless smoked lean
   bacon slices, coarsely chopped
1 garlic clove, crushed
7¼ cups ham or vegetable stock
1 bouquet garni (see Cook's Tip on
   page 19)
1 teaspoon dried oregano
4 ounces cooked ham, chopped
salt and ground black pepper

1. Drain the soaked split peas.
Melt the butter in a large saucepan,
add the onion, bacon, and garlic,
and cook over low heat for about
10 minutes or until the onion is soft.

2. Add the drained split peas to the
pan with the stock. Bring to a boil
and use a slotted spoon to remove
any scum that comes to the surface.
Add the bouquet garni and
oregano, and season with salt and
black pepper. Transfer to the slow
cooker, cover, and cook on high for
3–4 hours, until the peas are soft.

3. Let the soup cool a little. Then
process half the soup in a blender
or food processor until smooth.
Pour the soup into a saucepan and
reheat, and then add the ham and
check the seasoning. Ladle into
warmed bowls and sprinkle with
black pepper to serve.

COOK'S TIP

*Dried peas form the base of this
comforting soup. First, you need to
soak them overnight in about 4 cups
cold water. If you forget, put them
straight into a saucepan with the
water, bring to a boil, and cook for
1–2 minutes, and then let stand for
2 hours before using.*

Easy Chicken Casserole

Preparation Time 15 minutes • Cooking Time 5–6 hours on low • Serves 6 • Per Serving 323 calories, 18g fat (5g saturated), 17g carbohydrates, 900mg sodium • Gluten Free • Dairy Free • Easy

1 tablespoon sunflower oil
1 small chicken, about 3 pounds
1 fresh rosemary sprig
2 bay leaves
1 red onion, cut into wedges
2 carrots, cut into chunks
2 leeks, trimmed and cut into chunks
2 celery sticks, cut into chunks
12 baby new potatoes, halved if large
3½ cups hot chicken stock
8 ounces green beans, trimmed
salt and ground black pepper

1. Heat the oil in a large skillet over medium heat. Add the chicken and cook until browned all over. Put the chicken into the slow cooker, along with the herbs and all the vegetables except the green beans. Season well.

2. Pour in the hot stock, cover, and cook on low for 5–6 hours, until the chicken is cooked through. Add the beans for the last hour or cook separately in lightly salted boiling water and stir into the casserole once it's cooked. To test the chicken is cooked, pierce the thickest part of the leg with the tip of a sharp knife; the juices should run clear.

3. Remove the chicken and spoon the vegetables into six bowls. Carve the chicken and divide among the bowls, and then ladle the cooking liquid over the meat.

TRY SOMETHING DIFFERENT
Omit the baby new potatoes and serve with mashed potatoes.

Chicken Tagine with Apricots and Almonds

Preparation Time 10 minutes • Cooking Time 4–5 hours on low • Serves 4 • Per Serving 376 calories, 22g fat (4g saturated), 19g carbohydrates, 500g sodium • Gluten Free • Dairy Free • Easy

2 tablespoons olive oil
4 chicken thighs
1 onion, chopped
2 teaspoons ground cinnamon
2 tablespoons honey
¾ cup dried apricots
½ cup blanched almonds
½ cup hot chicken stock
salt and ground black pepper
slivered almonds to garnish
couscous to serve

1. Heat 1 tablespoon oil in a large skillet over medium heat. Add the chicken and cook for 5 minutes or until brown, and then transfer to the slow cooker.

2. Add the onion to the pan with the remaining oil and sauté for 10 minutes or until softened.

3. Add the cinnamon, honey, apricots, almonds, and hot stock to the onion and season well. Bring to a boil, and then transfer to the slow cooker, cover, and cook on low for 4–5 hours, until the chicken is tender and cooked through. Garnish with the slivered almonds and serve hot with couscous.

Spanish Chicken

Preparation Time 25 minutes, plus infusing • Cooking Time 1–2 hours on low • Serves 4 • Per Serving 671 calories, 28g fat (5g saturated), 70g carbohydrates, 800mg sodium • Gluten Free • Dairy Free • Easy

1 teaspoon ground turmeric

4½ cups hot chicken stock

2 tablespoons vegetable oil

4 boneless, skinless chicken thighs, coarsely diced

1 onion, chopped

1 red bell pepper, seeded and sliced

2 ounces chorizo sausage, diced

2 garlic cloves, crushed

1½ cups long-grain rice

1¼ cups frozen peas

salt and ground black pepper

3 tablespoons freshly chopped Italian parsley to garnish

crusty bread to serve

1. Add the turmeric to the hot stock and let steep for at least 5 minutes. Meanwhile, heat the oil in a large skillet over medium heat. Add the chicken and cook for 10 minutes or until golden brown, and then transfer to the slow cooker.

2. Add the onion to the skillet and sauté over medium heat for 5 minutes or until soft. Add the red bell pepper and chorizo and cook for another 5 minutes, and then add the garlic and cook for 1 minute.

3. Add the rice and mix well. Pour in the stock and peas and season. Transfer to the slow cooker and stir together. Cover and cook on low for 1–2 hours, until the rice is tender and the chicken is cooked through.

4. Check the seasoning and garnish with the parsley. Serve with some crusty bread.

Mexican Chili Con Carne

Preparation Time 5 minutes • Cooking Time 4–5 hours on low • Serves 4 • Per Serving 408 calories, 19g fat (7g saturated), 28g carbohydrates, 1,100mg sodium • Gluten Free • Dairy Free • Easy

2 tablespoons olive oil

1 pound ground round or sirloin beef

1 large onion, finely chopped

½–1 teaspoon each hot chili powder and ground cumin

3 tablespoons tomato paste

⅔ cup hot beef stock

1 (14½-ounce) can diced tomatoes with garlic (see Cook's Tips)

1 ounce semisweet chocolate

1 (15-ounce) can red kidney beans, drained and rinsed

1 cup freshly chopped cilantro

salt and ground black pepper

guacamole, salsa, sour cream, shredded cheese, tortilla chips, and pickled chilies to serve

1. Heat 1 tablespoon oil in a large skillet and sauté the ground beef for 10 minutes or until well browned, stirring to break up any lumps. Remove the beef from the pan with a slotted spoon and transfer to the slow cooker.

2. Add the remaining oil to the skillet, and then sauté the onion, stirring, for 10 minutes or until soft and golden brown.

3. Add the spices and cook for 1 minute. Then add the tomato paste, hot stock, and the tomatoes. Bring to a boil, and then stir into the beef in the slow cooker. Cover and cook on low for 4–5 hours.

4. Stir in the chocolate, kidney beans, and cilantro and season with salt and black pepper. Then let stand for 10 minutes.

5. Serve with guacamole, salsa, sour cream, shredded cheese, tortilla chips, and pickled chilies.

COOK'S TIPS

• *Instead of a can of tomatoes with garlic, use a can of diced tomatoes and 1 crushed garlic clove.*

• *Adding a little semisweet chocolate to chili con carne brings out the flavors of this tasty dish.*

Chicken with Chorizo and Beans

Preparation Time 10 minutes • Cooking Time 4–5 hours on low • Serves 6 • Per Serving 690 calories, 41g fat (12g saturated), 33g carbohydrates, 2,600mg sodium • Dairy Free • Easy

1 tablespoon olive oil

12 chicken pieces (drumsticks and thighs)

6 ounces chorizo sausage, cubed

1 onion, finely chopped

2 large garlic cloves, crushed

1 teaspoon mild chili powder

3 red bell peppers, seeded and coarsely chopped

1¾ cups canned tomato puree or tomato sauce

2 tablespoons tomato paste

⅔ cup hot chicken stock

2 (15-ounce) cans lima beans, drained and rinsed

8 ounces new potatoes, quartered

1 small bunch of fresh thyme

1 bay leaf

1 (6-ounce) package baby leaf spinach

1. Heat the oil in a large saucepan over medium heat. Add the chicken and cook until browned all over, and then transfer to the slow cooker.

2. Add the chorizo to the pan and sauté for 2–3 minutes, until its oil starts to run. Add the onion, garlic, and chili powder and sauté over low heat for 5 minutes or until the onion is soft.

3. Add the red bell peppers and cook for 2–3 minutes, until soft. Stir in the tomato puree or sauce, tomato paste, hot stock, lima beans, potatoes, thyme sprigs, and bay leaf. Bring to a boil, and then add to the chicken. Cover and cook on low for 4–5 hours, until the chicken is cooked through.

4. Remove the thyme and bay leaf, and then stir in the spinach until it wilts. Serve immediately.

TRY SOMETHING DIFFERENT

Use mixed beans instead of the lima beans.

Beef Goulash

Preparation Time 30 minutes • Cooking Time 8–10 hours on low • Serves 6 • Per Serving 726 calories, 44g fat (16g saturated), 21g carbohydrates, 1,600mg sodium • Easy

2¼ **pounds boneless beef chuck or beef round, cut into 1¼-inch cubes**

2 **tablespoons seasoned all-purpose flour**

3 **tablespoons vegetable oil**

5 **onions, chopped**

8 **ounces pancetta or bacon, diced**

2 **garlic cloves, crushed**

¼ **cup paprika**

2 **teaspoons dried mixed herbs**

1 **(14½-ounce) can peeled plum tomatoes**

⅔ **cup hot beef stock**

⅔ **cup sour cream**

salt and ground black pepper

freshly chopped Italian parsley, to garnish

noodles to serve

1. Toss the beef in the flour to coat and shake off any excess.

2. Heat 2 tablespoons oil in a large saucepan and quickly cook the meat in small batches until browned on all sides. Transfer to the slow cooker.

3. Heat the remaining oil in the pan, add the onions, and sauté gently for 5–7 minutes, until starting to soften and turn golden brown. Add the pancetta or bacon and sauté over high heat until crispy. Stir in the garlic and paprika and cook, stirring, for 1 minute.

4. Add the herbs, tomatoes, and hot stock and bring to a boil. Stir into the beef in the slow cooker, cover, and cook on low for 8–10 hours, until tender.

5. Check the seasoning, and then stir in the sour cream. Garnish with parsley and serve with noodles.

Beef and Guinness Stew

Preparation Time 15 minutes • Cooking Time 8–10 hours on low • Serves 6 • Per Serving 526 calories, 29g fat (10g saturated), 10g carbohydrates, 400mg sodium • Dairy Free • Easy

3 pounds beef shank or chuck shoulder steak, cut into 1¼-inch cubes
2 tablespoons seasoned all-purpose flour
¼ cup vegetable oil
2 medium onions, sliced
4 medium carrots, cut into chunks
1 cup Guinness stout*
1¼ cups hot beef stock
2 bay leaves
1½ pounds new potatoes, halved if large
2 tablespoons freshly chopped Italian parsley
salt and ground black pepper

1. Toss the beef in the flour to coat and shake off any excess. Heat the oil in a large saucepan until hot. Add a handful of beef and cook until well browned. Remove with a slotted spoon, transfer to the slow cooker, and repeat until all the meat is browned.

2. Add the onions and carrots to the pan and cook for 10 minutes or until browned. Add the Guinness, scraping the bottom to loosen the sediment, and then stir in the hot stock. Add the bay leaves and potatoes and bring to a boil. Pour over the beef in the slow cooker, cover, and cook on low for 8–10 hours, until the meat is tender.

3. Stir in the parsley, season to taste, and serve.

* This recipe is not suitable for children because it contains alcohol.

Curried Lamb with Lentils

Preparation Time 15 minutes, plus marinating • Cooking Time 5–6 hours on low • Serves 4 • Per Serving 478 calories, 22g fat (7g saturated), 36g carbohydrates, 300mg sodium • Gluten Free • Dairy Free • Easy

1 pound lean lamb on the bone, cut into 8 pieces (ask your butcher to do this), trimmed of fat

1 teaspoon ground cumin

1 teaspoon ground turmeric

2 garlic cloves, crushed

1 medium red chili, seeded and chopped (see Cook's Tip on page 15)

1-inch piece fresh ginger, peeled and grated

2 tablespoons vegetable oil

1 onion, chopped

1 (14½-ounce) can diced tomatoes

2 tablespoons vinegar

1 cup boiling water

1 cup red lentils, rinsed

salt and ground black pepper

fresh cilantro sprigs to garnish

arugula salad to serve

1. Put the lamb into a shallow sealable container and add the spices, garlic, chili, ginger, salt, and black pepper. Stir well to mix, and then cover and chill for at least 30 minutes.

2. Heat the oil in a large saucepan, add the onion, and cook over low heat for 5 minutes. Add the marinated lamb and cook for 10 minutes, turning regularly, or until the meat is evenly browned.

3. Add the tomatoes, vinegar, lentils, and the boiling water and bring to a boil. Season well. Transfer to the slow cooker, cover, and cook on low for 5–6 hours, until the lamb is tender.

4. Serve hot, garnished with cilantro, with an arugula salad.

Spiced Bean and Vegetable Stew

Preparation Time 15 minutes • Cooking Time 2–3 hours on low • Serves 6 • Per Serving 262 calories, 7g fat (1g saturated), 44g carbohydrates, 1,300mg sodium • Vegetarian • Gluten Free • Dairy Free • Easy

3 tablespoons olive oil
2 small onions, sliced
2 garlic cloves, crushed
1 tablespoon sweet paprika
1 small dried red chili, seeded and finely chopped
3 sweet potatoes (about 1½ pounds), cubed
1 butternut squash, peeled, seeded, and cut into chunks
4 ounces okra, trimmed
2 cups canned tomato puree or tomato sauce
1 (14½-ounce) can navy or cannellini beans, drained and rinsed
2 cups hot vegetable stock
salt and ground black pepper

1. Heat the oil in a large saucepan over gentle heat. Add the onions and garlic and cook for 5 minutes.

2. Stir in the paprika and chili and cook for 2 minutes. Then add the sweet potatoes, squash, okra, tomato puree or sauce, beans, and hot stock. Season generously with salt and black pepper and bring to a boil.

3. Transfer to the slow cooker, cover, and cook on low for 2–3 hours, until the vegetables are tender.

TRY SOMETHING DIFFERENT
Instead of paprika, use 1 teaspoon each ground cumin and ground coriander. Garnish with freshly chopped cilantro.

Mushroom and Bean Stew

Preparation Time 15 minutes • Cooking Time 2–3 hours on low • Serves 6 • Per Serving 280 calories, 10g fat (1g saturated), 34g carbohydrates, 1,300mg sodium • Vegetarian • Dairy Free • Easy

3 tablespoons olive oil

1½ pounds cremini mushrooms, coarsely chopped

1 large onion, finely chopped

2 tablespoons all-purpose flour

2 tablespoons mild curry paste

⅔ cup dry white wine*

1 (14½-ounce) can diced tomatoes

2 tablespoons tomato paste

3 cups drained and rinsed, canned mixed beans, such as kidney beans, pinto beans, and chickpeas

3 tablespoons mango chutney

3 tablespoons freshly chopped cilantro and mint

1. Heat the oil in a large saucepan over low heat and sauté the mushrooms and onion until the onion is soft and dark golden brown. Stir in the flour and curry paste and cook for 1–2 minutes. Add the wine, tomatoes, tomato paste, and beans.

2. Bring to a boil, and then transfer to the slow cooker. Cover and cook on low for 2–3 hours.

3. Stir in the chutney and herbs and serve.

This recipe is not suitable for children because it contains alcohol.

Lentils with Red Pepper

Preparation Time 10 minutes • Cooking Time 3–4 hours on high, plus standing • Serves 4 • Per Serving 296 calories, 5g fat (1g saturated), 47g carbohydrates, 100mg sodium • Vegetarian • Gluten Free • Dairy Free • Easy

1 tablespoon olive oil
1 large onion, finely chopped
2 celery sticks, diced
2 carrots, diced
2 bay leaves, torn
1½ cups green lentils
2½ cups hot vegetable stock

1 marinated red pepper, drained
 and chopped
2 tablespoons freshly chopped
 Italian parsley, plus extra to
 garnish
ground black pepper

1. Heat the oil in a saucepan, add the onion, and cook over low heat for 15 minutes or until soft. Add the celery, carrots, and bay leaves and cook for 2 minutes.

2. Add the lentils with the hot stock and stir everything together. Transfer to the slow cooker, cover, and cook on high for 3–4 hours.

3. Stir in the marinated red pepper and parsley and season with black pepper. Let stand for 10 minutes. Then garnish with extra parsley.

Braised Red Cabbage

Preparation Time 10 minutes • Cooking Time 2–3 hours on low • Serves 8 • Per Serving 50 calories, trace fat, 11g carbohydrates, trace sodium • Vegetarian • Gluten Free • Dairy Free • Easy

7 cups shredded red cabbage
1 red onion, finely chopped
1 Granny Smith apple, peeled, cored, and chopped
2 tablespoons packed light brown sugar
1 cinnamon stick

a pinch of ground cloves
¼ teaspoon freshly grated nutmeg
2 tablespoons red wine vinegar
2 tablespoons red wine*
juice of 1 orange
2 tablespoons cold water
salt and ground black pepper

1. Put all the ingredients into the slow cooker and stir to mix well. Cover and cook on low for 2–3 hours.

2. When the cabbage is tender, discard the cinnamon stick. Serve at once, or cool, put into a bowl, cover, and chill the cabbage overnight.

3. To reheat, put the cabbage into a saucepan, add the cold water, and cover with a tight-fitting lid. Bring to a boil, and then reduce the heat and simmer for 25 minutes.

* This recipe is not suitable for children because it contains alcohol.

SWEET
TREATS

Winter Fruit Compote

Preparation Time 10 minutes • Cooking Time 3–4 hours on Low • Serves 6 • Per Serving 139 calories, trace fat, 26g carbohydrates, 100mg sodium • Vegetarian • Gluten Free • Dairy Free • Easy

½ cup dried pears
½ cup dried figs
½ cup dried apricots
½ cup prunes
1 star anise
½ cinnamon stick
1¼ cups apple juice
1¼ cups dry white wine*
light brown sugar, to taste
crème fraîche or thick Greek-style
   yogurt to serve

1. Put the dried fruits into a slow cooker with the star anise and cinnamon stick.

2. Put the apple juice and wine into a saucepan and bring to a boil. Pour over the fruit, cover, and cook on Low for 3–4 hours, until plump and tender.

3. Turn the compote into a bowl. Taste the cooking liquid for sweetness, adding a little sugar, if necessary. Let cool to room temperature.

4. Serve the compote with crème fraîche or thick Greek-style yogurt.

* This recipe is not suitable for children because it contains alcohol.

TRY SOMETHING DIFFERENT
Replace the figs with dried apple slices and the pears with raisins.

Hot Spiced Fruit Salad

Preparation Time 10 minutes • Cooking Time 1½ hours • Serves 6 • Per Serving 185 calories,
1g fat (0g saturated), 44g carbohydrates, 100mg sodium • Vegetarian • Gluten Free • Dairy Free • Easy

3 apples, cored and chopped
3 pears, cored and chopped
12 dried apricots
12 dried figs
juice of 2 large oranges
⅔ cup apple juice
a pinch of ground cinnamon
1 star anise

1. Preheat the oven to 350°F. Put the apples and pears into a roasting pan with the apricots, figs, orange juice, apple juice, ground cinnamon, and star anise. Stir, cover with aluminum foil, and bake in the oven for 1 hour.

2. Remove the foil and bake for another 30 minutes. Discard the star anise and serve.

TRY SOMETHING DIFFERENT
Prunes or ½ cup dried cranberries can be substituted for the figs.

Drunken Pears

Preparation Time 15 minutes • Cooking Time 50 minutes • Serves 4 • Per Serving 305 calories, trace fat, 52g carbohydrates, 0mg sodium • Vegetarian • Gluten Free • Dairy Free • Easy

4 Bartlett or Comice pears
¾ cup granulated sugar
1¼ cups red wine*
⅔ cup sloe gin
1¼ cups water
1 cinnamon stick
zest of 1 orange
6 star anise
Greek yogurt or whipped cream
  to serve (optional)

1. Peel the pears, cut out the calyx at the bottom of each, and leave the stems intact. Put the sugar, wine, sloe gin, and water into a small saucepan and heat gently until the sugar dissolves.

2. Bring to a boil and add the cinnamon stick, orange zest, and star anise. Add the pears. Then cover and poach over low heat for 30 minutes or until tender.

3. Remove the pears with a slotted spoon, and continue to heat the liquid until it has reduced to about ¾ cup or until syrupy. Pour the syrup over the pears. Serve warm or chilled with Greek yogurt or whipped cream, if desired.

* This recipe is not suitable for children because it contains alcohol.

GET AHEAD
To prepare ahead *Complete the recipe, cool, cover, and chill for up to three days.*

Sticky Toffee Pudding

Preparation Time 20 minutes • Cooking Time 25–30 minutes, plus resting • Serves 4 • Per Serving 565 calories, 38g fat (21g saturated), 53g carbohydrates, 900mg sodium • Vegetarian • Easy

1 tablespoon light corn syrup

1 tablespoon molasses

½ cup (1 stick) butter, softened

¼ cup pecans or walnuts, finely ground

½ cup all-purpose flour

½ cup baking powder

⅔ cup superfine sugar or granulated sugar

2 extra-large eggs, beaten

cream or custard to serve

1. Preheat the oven to 350°F. Put the syrup, molasses, and 2 tablespoons butter into a bowl and beat until smooth. Divide the batter among four ⅔-cup timbales or ramekins and set aside.

2. Put the nuts into a bowl, sift in the flour and baking powder, and mix together well.

3. Put the remaining butter and the sugar into a food processor and blend briefly. (Alternatively, use an electric mixer.) Add the eggs and the flour mixture and blend or mix again for 30 seconds. Spoon the mixture into the timbales or ramekins, covering the syrup mixture on the bottom. Bake for 25–30 minutes, until risen and golden brown.

4. Remove the cakes from the oven and let rest for 5 minutes, and then unmold onto warmed plates. Serve immediately with cream or custard.

Chocolate Bread Pudding

Preparation Time 20 minutes, plus chilling • Cooking Time 55–75 minutes • Serves 6 • Per Serving 390 calories, 17g fat (6g saturated), 51g carbohydrates, 700mg sodium • Vegetarian • A Little Effort

½ loaf **French bread**

4 ounces **milk chocolate, coarsely chopped**

1¾ cups **freshly prepared custard or vanilla pudding**

⅔ cup **low-fat milk**

1 **extra-large egg, beaten**

butter to grease

1 tablespoon **raw sugar**

½ cup **finely chopped walnuts**

2 ounces **semisweet or milk chocolate, broken into chunks**

light cream to serve (optional)

1. Coarsely chop the French bread and put it into a large bowl. Put the chopped milk chocolate in a saucepan with the custard or pudding and the milk over low heat. Stir gently until the chocolate has melted. Beat in the egg.

2. Pour the chocolate mixture over the bread, stir well to coat. Cover and chill for at least 4 hours.

3. Preheat the oven to 350°F. Spoon the soaked bread into a buttered 1½-quart, 3-inch deep, ovenproof dish, and bake for 30–40 minutes.

4. Sprinkle with the sugar, walnuts, and chocolate chunks. Put the dish back in the oven for 20–30 minutes, until lightly set. Serve the dessert warm, with light cream, if desired.

TRY SOMETHING DIFFERENT
Instead of French bread, use crescent rolls or challah bread for a richer dessert.

Panettone Pudding

Preparation Time 20 minutes, plus soaking • Cooking Time 35–45 minutes • Serves 6 • Per Serving 581 calories, 29g fat (16g saturated), 73g carbohydrates, 900mg sodium • Vegetarian • Easy

4 tablespoons butter, at room temperature, plus extra to grease

1 loaf panettone (see Cook's Tip), cut into slices about ¼ inch thick

3 extra-large eggs, beaten

¾ cup superfine sugar or granulated sugar

1¼ cups whole milk

⅔ cup heavy cream

grated zest of 1 orange

1. Butter a 2-quart ovenproof dish. Lightly butter the panettone slices, and then tear them into pieces and arrange in the dish.

2. Mix the eggs with the sugar in a large bowl, and then whisk in the milk, cream, and orange zest. Pour the mixture over the buttered panettone and let soak for 20 minutes. Preheat the oven to 325°F.

3. Put the dish in a roasting pan and pour in enough hot water to come halfway up the sides. Bake for 35–45 minutes, until the dessert is just set in the middle and golden.

COOK'S TIP

Panettone is a yeasted fruit cake that is a traditional Christmas treat in Italy and is most widely available around Christmas time. If you can't find it, use brioche, challah bread, or cinnamon and raisin bread.

Rice Pudding

Preparation Time 5 minutes • Cooking Time 1½ hours • Serves 6 • Per Serving 239 calories, 8g fat (5g saturated), 34g carbohydrates, 200mg sodium • Vegetarian • Gluten Free • Easy

butter to grease
½ cup short-grain rice
4½ cups whole milk
¼ cup superfine sugar or granulated sugar
1 teaspoon vanilla extract
grated zest of 1 orange (optional)
freshly grated nutmeg to taste

1. Preheat the oven to 350°F. Lightly butter a 2-quart ovenproof dish. Add the rice, milk, sugar, vanilla extract, and orange zest, if using, and stir everything together. Grate the nutmeg over the top of the mixture.

2. Bake the dessert in the middle of the oven for 1½ hours or until the top is golden brown.

Pecan Pie

Preparation Time 25 minutes, plus chilling • Cooking Time 1 hour 10 minutes, plus cooling • Serves 8 •
Per Serving 549 calories, 40g fat (16g saturated), 45g carbohydrates, 400mg sodium • Vegetarian • Easy

PIE DOUGH

1½ cups all-purpose flour, plus
   extra to dust
pinch of salt
6 tablespoons chilled butter, cubed
½ cup confectioners' sugar
1 large egg
1½ teaspoons water
ice-cream to serve

FOR THE FILLING

½ cup (1 stick) butter
¼ cup honey
2 tablespoons granulated sugar
⅓ cup packed dark brown sugar
3 tablespoons heavy cream
grated zest of 1 small lemon
1 teaspoon vanilla extract
1¼ cups pecans

1. To make the pie crust, sift the all-purpose flour and a pinch of salt into a bowl and add the butter. Using your fingertips or a pastry cutter, rub or cut the butter into the flour until the mixture resembles fine bread crumbs. Using a fork, mix in the sugar, egg, and water until the mixture holds together; add a little more water, if necessary.

2. Gather the dough in your hands and knead lightly. Form into a ball, wrap tightly in plastic wrap, and chill for at least 30 minutes before using. (This "relaxes" the pastry and prevents shrinkage when it is baked.)

3. Roll the pie dough on a lightly floured surface into a 12-inch diameter circle and use to line an 8-inch diameter, 1-inch deep, loose-bottom fluted tart pan. Put the pan on a baking sheet and chill for 20 minutes.

4. Meanwhile, preheat the oven to 400°F. Line the pastry shell with parchment paper and pie weights or dried beans and bake for 15 minutes. Remove the paper and weights, and then return the pastry shell to the oven for another 10 minutes. Reduce the oven temperature to 300°F.

5. To make the filling, melt the butter with the honey and sugars over low heat, bring to a boil without stirring, and simmer for 2–3 minutes. Remove from the heat, stir in the cream, lemon zest, vanilla extract, and nuts, and let cool for 15 minutes.

6. Pour the pecan mixture into the pastry shell. Bake for 40 minutes or until the mixture begins to simmer in the middle (cover with aluminum foil if it gets too dark). Serve warm with ice cream.

GET AHEAD

To prepare ahead Complete the recipe, and then cool and store in an airtight container for up to two days.
To use Heat the pie at 350°F for 15–20 minutes.

FREEZING TIP

To freeze Complete the recipe, and then cool, wrap, and freeze the pie in its pan.
To use Reheat the pie from frozen at 350°F for 25 minutes or until warm. Cover with aluminum foil if it gets too dark.

Lemon Meringue Pie

Preparation Time 30 minutes • Cooking Time about 1 hour, plus standing • Serves 8 • Per Serving 692 calories, 36g fat (21g saturated), 83g carbohydrates, 600mg sodium • Vegetarian • Easy

**9-inch store-bought pie crust,
    thawed if frozen**

FOR THE FILLING
**7 large eggs, 4 separated,
    at room temperature**
finely grated zest of 3 lemons
**¾ cup freshly squeezed lemon
    juice (about 4 lemons), strained**
1 (14-ounce) can condensed milk
⅔ cup heavy cream
1 cup confectioners' sugar

1. Preheat the oven to 350°F. To make the filling, put 4 egg yolks into a bowl with the 3 whole eggs. Add the lemon zest and juice and whisk lightly. Mix in the condensed milk and cream.

2. Pour the filling into the pie crust and bake for 30 minutes or until just set in the center. Put to one side to cool while you prepare the meringue. Increase the oven temperature to 400°F.

3. For the meringue, beat the egg whites and sugar together in a double boiler or a heatproof bowl set over a saucepan of gently simmering water, using an electric mixer, for 10 minutes or until shiny and thick. Remove from the heat and beat at a low speed for another 5–10 minutes until the bowl is cool.

4. Pile the meringue on top of the lemon filling and swirl with a frosting spatula to form peaks. Bake for 5–10 minutes, until the meringue is tinged brown. Let stand for about 1 hour, and then serve.

Plum Cobbler

Preparation Time 25 minutes • Cooking Time 40 minutes • Serves 6 • Per Serving 451 calories,
15g fat (9g saturated), 76g carbohydrates, 300mg sodium • Vegetarian • Easy

**14 plums (about 2 pounds), halved
   and pitted**
**¾ cup superfine sugar or
   granulated sugar, plus
   3 tablespoons**
1 tablespoon cornstarch
1¾ cups all-purpose flour
1¾ teaspoons baking powder
**6 tablespoons chilled unsalted
   butter, diced**
**¾ cup buttermilk or whole plain
   yogurt**

1. Preheat the oven to 400°F. Cut the plums into chunky wedges. Put into an ovenproof dish measuring 10 × 7 × 3 inches and toss together with 3 tablespoons sugar and the cornstarch.

2. Process the flour, baking powder, butter, and ½ cup sugar in a food processor until the mixture forms fine crumbs. (Alternatively, rub the butter into the flour by hand or using a pastry cutter, and then stir in the sugar.) Add the buttermilk or yogurt and blend for a few seconds until just combined.

3. Sprinkle clumps of the dough over the plums, leaving some of the fruit exposed. Sprinkle the cobbler with the remaining sugar and bake for 40 minutes or until the fruit is tender and the topping is a pale golden brown.

**TRY SOMETHING
DIFFERENT**
*Toss the plums with the grated zest
of ½ orange before baking, and
add the grated zest of the remaining
½ orange to the cobbler mixture
with the buttermilk.*

Sugar-Crusted Fruit Pie

Preparation Time 30 minutes, plus 30 minutes chilling • Cooking Time about 40 minutes, plus cooling • Serves 4 •
Per Serving 673 calories, 38g fat (17g saturated), 79g carbohydrates, 500mg sodium • Vegetarian • Easy

½ cup hazelnuts

2 cups pitted cherries

½ cup superfine sugar or
  granulated sugar

1¼ cups all-purpose flour, plus
  extra to dust

½ cup (1 stick) butter

3 Pippin apples, peeled, cored,
  and quartered

1. Spread the hazelnuts over a baking sheet. Toast under a hot broiler until golden brown, turning them frequently. Put the hazelnuts in a clean dish towel and rub off the skins. Let cool.

2. Put the cherries into a bowl with 2 tablespoons of the sugar. Cover and set aside. For the hazelnut dough, put ⅓ cup hazelnuts into a food processor with the flour, and pulse to a powder. Remove and set aside. In the food processor, process the butter with ¼ cup sugar. Add the flour mixture and pulse until it forms a dough. Turn out onto a lightly floured surface and knead lightly, and then wrap and chill for 30 minutes. If the dough cracks, just work it together.

3. Preheat the oven to 350°F. Cut the apples into small chunks and put into a 1-quart oval pie plate. Spoon the cherries on top. Roll out the dough on a lightly floured surface to about ¼-inch thick. Cut into ½-inch strips. Dampen the edge of the pie plate with a little water and press a few of the strips onto the rim to cover it. Dampen the pastry rim. Put the remaining strips over the cherries to create a lattice pattern.

4. Brush the pastry with water and sprinkle with the remaining sugar. Bake for 30–35 minutes until the pastry is golden brown. Set aside to cool for 15 minutes.

5. Chop the remaining toasted hazelnuts and sprinkle them over the pie. Serve warm.

GET AHEAD

To prepare ahead *Complete the recipe to the end of step 4, and then cool, wrap, and chill for up to three days.*
To use *Bake at 350°F for 20–25 minutes to heat through. Complete the recipe.*

FREEZING TIP

To freeze *Complete the recipe to the end of step 3, and then wrap and freeze.*
To use *Brush the pastry with egg and sprinkle the extra sugar on top. Bake from frozen at 350°F for 40–45 minutes until golden brown. Complete the recipe.*

Baked Orange Custard

Preparation Time 10 minutes, plus infusing and cooling • Cooking Time 50 minutes or 1 hour 10 minutes, plus chilling • Serves 6 • Per Serving 268 calories, 20g fat (10g saturated), 18g carbohydrates, 200mg sodium • Gluten Free • Easy

finely grated zest of 1 orange

2 cups milk

⅔ cup heavy cream

½ cup honey (see Cook's Tips)

2 extra-large eggs, plus 4 extra-large yolks

2 tablespoons superfine sugar or granulated sugar

slivers of orange zest to garnish

1. Put the orange zest, milk, and cream into a saucepan, and bring to a boil. Set aside for 30 minutes to steep.

2. Preheat the oven to 300°F. Warm a 1-quart soufflé dish or six ⅔-cup coffee cups in the oven. Bring the honey to a boil in a small, heavy saucepan. Simmer for 2–3 minutes, until it begins to caramelize (see Cook's Tips). Pour the caramel into the warmed dish or cups and rotate to coat the bottom. Set aside to cool and harden.

3. Put the eggs, yolks, and sugar into a bowl and beat together until smooth. Add the steeped milk mixture, stir until well combined, and then strain into the dish or cups. Put the dish or cups into a roasting pan, adding enough hot water to come halfway up the side(s). Bake for 1 hour 10 minutes for the soufflé dish or 45–50 minutes for the coffee cups until just set in the middle (see Cook's Tips). Cool and chill for at least 6 hours or overnight. Decorate with orange zest.

COOK'S TIPS

• *Look for a mild flower honey, such as lavender or orange blossom; a strong honey will be overpowering.*

• *The honey needs to be cooked to a golden-brown caramel—any darker and it will become bitter.*

• *The custard may still be wobbly after cooking, but don't worry, it gets firm on cooling and chilling.*

Caramel Cheesecake

Preparation Time 15 minutes, plus chilling • Cooking Time 45–60 minutes, plus cooling • Serves 10 •
Per Serving 379 calories, 24g fat (13g saturated), 34g carbohydrates, 1,100mg sodium • Vegetarian • Easy

11 ounces graham crackers (about 44 crackers)
½ cup (1 stick) unsalted butter, melted

FOR THE FILLING
2 cups cream cheese
½ cup heavy cream
juice of ½ lemon
3 large eggs, beaten
¼ cup superfine sugar or granulated sugar
⅓ cup dulce de leche (caramel sauce), plus extra to drizzle

1. Put the crackers into a food processor and process until they resemble fine crumbs. (Alternatively, put them into a plastic bag and crush with a rolling pin.) Transfer to a bowl. Add the butter and blend briefly, or stir in, to combine. Transfer the crumb mixture to an 8-inch springform cake pan and press evenly into the bottom and up the sides. Chill for about 1 hour or until firm.

2. Preheat the oven to 400°F. To make the filling, put the cream cheese and cream into a food processor or blender and process until smooth. Add the lemon juice, eggs, sugar, and caramel sauce, and then blend again until smooth. Pour into the chilled crumb crust and bake for 10 minutes. Reduce the oven temperature to 350°F, and then bake for 45 minutes or until set and golden brown.

3. Turn off the oven and let the cheesecake stand inside, with the door ajar, until it is cool. When completely cool, chill for at least 2 hours, until the crust is firm.

4. To remove the cheesecake from the pan, run a knife around the edge of the cake. Open the pan carefully, and then use a frosting spatula to ease the cheesecake out. Cut into wedges, put on a serving plate and drizzle with caramel sauce.

COOK'S TIP
To slice the cheesecake easily, use a sharp knife dipped into boiling water and then wiped dry.

Chocolate Brownie

Preparation Time 15 minutes • Cooking Time 20–25 minutes, plus cooling • Cuts into 16 brownies •
Per Brownie 352 calories, 25g fat (13g saturated), 29g carbohydrates, 300mg sodium • Easy

**1 cup (2 sticks) butter, plus extra
  to grease**
**8 ounces good-quality semisweet
  chocolate, broken into pieces**
**4 ounces white chocolate, broken
  into pieces**
4 large eggs
1 cup packed light brown sugar
1 teaspoon vanilla extract
½ cup all-purpose flour, sifted
¼ teaspoon baking powder
**1 tablespoon unsweetened cocoa
  powder, sifted, plus extra to dust**
⅔ cup chopped pecans
a pinch of salt
a little confectioners' sugar to dust

1. Preheat the oven to 400°F. Grease an 8-inch-square, shallow cake pan and line the bottom with parchment paper. Melt the butter and semisweet chocolate in a double boiler or a heatproof bowl set over a saucepan of gently simmering water, making sure the bottom of the bowl doesn't touch the water. Remove the chocolate and put to one side.

2. In a clean double boiler or separate bowl, melt the white chocolate as above and put to one side.

3. Put the eggs into a separate large bowl. Add the brown sugar and vanilla extract and beat together until the mixture is pale and thick.

4. Add the flour, baking powder, cocoa powder, pecans, and a pinch of salt to the bowl, and then carefully pour in the semisweet chocolate mixture. Using a large metal spoon, gently fold the ingredients together to make a smooth batter; if you fold too roughly, the chocolate will seize up and become unusable.

5. Pour the brownie batter into the prepared pan. Spoon dollops of the white chocolate over the brownie mix, and then swirl a toothpick through it several times to create a marbled effect.

6. Bake for 20–25 minutes. The brownie should be fudgy inside and the top should be cracked and crispy. Let cool in the pan.

7. Transfer the brownies to a board and cut into 16 individual brownies. To serve, dust with a little confectioners' sugar and cocoa powder.

TO STORE
Complete the recipe to the end of step 6, and then store in an airtight container. It will keep for up to one week. Complete the recipe to serve.

TRY SOMETHING DIFFERENT
Try making these brownies without butter. Believe it or not, this recipe will still work, but you'll need to eat them within an hour of taking them out of the oven; the fat is what makes cakes moist and allows for them to be stored.

Quick Apple Tart

Preparation Time 10 minutes • Cooking Time 20–25 minutes • Serves 8 • Per Serving 221 calories, 12g fat (0g saturated), 29g carbohydrates, 400mg sodium • Vegetarian • Easy

1 sheet ready-to-bake puff pastry

3 Pippin apples, cored, thinly sliced, and tossed in the juice of 1 lemon

confectioners' sugar to dust

1. Preheat the oven to 400°F. Put the pastry on an 11 x 15-inch baking sheet and roll lightly with a rolling pin to smooth down the pastry. Score lightly around the edge to create a 1¼-inch border.

2. Arrange the apple slices on top of the pastry, within the border. Turn the edge of the pastry halfway over, so that it reaches the edge of the apples, and then press down and use your fingers to crimp the edge. Dust heavily with confectioners' sugar.

3. Bake in the oven for 20–25 minutes, until the pastry is cooked and the sugar has caramelized. Serve warm, dusted with more confectioners' sugar.

Strawberry Brûlée

Preparation Time 15 minutes, plus cooling and chilling • Cooking Time 5 minutes • Serves 4 •
Per Serving 240 calories, 10g fat (5g saturated), 35g carbohydrates, 200mg sodium • Vegetarian •
Gluten Free • Easy

**1¾ cups hulled and sliced
strawberries**
2 teaspoons confectioners' sugar
1 vanilla bean
1¾ cups Greek yogurt
**½ cup superfine sugar or
granulated sugar**

1. Divide the strawberries among
four ramekins and sprinkle with the
confectioners' sugar.

2. Scrape the seeds from the vanilla
bean and stir into the yogurt. Then
spread the mixture evenly over the
strawberries.

3. Preheat the broiler to high.
Sprinkle the superfine or granulated
sugar evenly over the yogurt until
it's well covered.

4. Put the ramekins on a baking
sheet or into the broiler pan and
broil until the sugar turns dark
brown and caramelizes. Let sit for
15 minutes or until the caramel is
cool enough to eat, or chill for up
to 2 hours before serving.

**TRY SOMETHING
DIFFERENT**
*Use raspberries or blueberries
instead of the strawberries.*

Decadent Chocolate Cake

Preparation Time 30 minutes • Cooking Time 1½ hours, plus cooling and setting • Cuts into 12 slices •
Per Slice 687 calories, 49g fat (23g saturated), 54g carbohydrates, 700mg sodium • Easy

1 cup (2 sticks) unsalted butter,
  softened, plus extra to grease
12 ounces semisweet chocolate,
  broken into pieces
1 cup superfine sugar or
  granulated sugar
2½ cups ground almonds (almond
  meal)
8 extra-large eggs, separated
2¼ cups fresh brown bread
  crumbs
¼ cup apricot preserves (optional)

FOR THE GANACHE

6 ounces semisweet chocolate,
  broken into pieces
6 tablespoons butter, softened
¼ cup heavy cream

1. Preheat the oven to 350°F. Grease a 9-inch springform pan and line with parchment paper.

2. Melt the chocolate in a double boiler or a heatproof bowl set over a saucepan of gently simmering water, making sure the bottom of the bowl doesn't touch the water. Remove the chocolate and set aside.

3. Put the butter and sugar into a large bowl and beat until light and creamy. Add the almonds, egg yolks, and bread crumbs. Beat well until thoroughly mixed. Slowly add the chocolate and carefully stir it in. Do not overmix because the chocolate may seize up and become unworkable.

4. Put the egg whites into a clean, grease-free bowl and beat until stiff peaks form. Add half the whites to the chocolate mixture and, using a large metal spoon, fold in lightly. Carefully fold in the remainder. Pour into the prepared pan and level the surface.

5. Bake for 1 hour 20 minutes or until the cake is firm to the touch and a toothpick inserted into the center comes out clean. Cool in the pan for 5 minutes, and then transfer to a wire rack for 2–3 hours to cool completely.

6. Put the preserves, if using, into a saucepan and melt over low heat. Brush it over the top and sides of the cake.

7. To make the ganache: Melt the chocolate, butter, and cream in a double boiler or heatproof bowl set over a saucepan of gently simmering water, making sure the bottom of the bowl doesn't touch the water. Stir just once until smooth. Either raise the cake off the counter on the upturned pan or put it (still on the rack) on a tray to catch the drips. Pour the ganache into the center and tip the cake to let it run down the sides evenly, or spread it with a frosting spatula.

Index